It's a brilliant development from CGP!

GCSE OCR B Geography is all about people and the natural world...
and naturally there are plenty of tricky questions in the new Grade 9-1 exams.

Not to worry. This CGP book is bursting with exam-style practice for every
topic — perfect for making sure you're ready for the real thing.

There's even a section of practice for those tricky questions from
the new Geographical Exploration paper. Everything you
need to shore up your knowledge and coast through the exams.

CGP — still the best! ☺

Our sole aim here at CGP is to produce the highest quality books —
carefully written, immaculately presented and dangerously close to being funny.

Then we work our socks off to get them out to you
— at the cheapest possible prices.

Contents

✓ Use the tick boxes to check off the topics you've completed.

Component 1: Our Natural World

Topic 1 — Global Hazards

Topic 2 — Changing Climate

Topic 3 — Distinctive Landscapes

Topic 4 — Sustaining Ecosystems

Component 2: People and Society

Topic 5 — Urban Futures

Published by CGP

Editors:
Claire Boulter, David Maliphant, Claire Plowman, Hannah Roscoe, David Ryan.

With thanks to Karen Wells and Ruth Wheeler for the proofreading.

With thanks to Ana Pungartnik for copyright research.

ISBN: 978 1 78294 619 9

Clipart from Corel®
Printed by Elanders Ltd, Newcastle upon Tyne

Based on the classic CGP style created by Richard Parsons.

How to Use this Book

- Hold the book <u>upright</u>, approximately <u>50 cm</u> from your face, ensuring that the text looks like <u>this</u>, not s̅i̅ɥ̅ʇ̅. Alternatively, place the book on a <u>horizontal</u> surface (e.g. a table or desk) and sit adjacent to the book, at a distance which doesn't make the text too small to read.

- In case of emergency, press the two halves of the book together <u>firmly</u> in order to close.

- Before attempting to use this book, familiarise yourself with the following <u>safety information</u>:

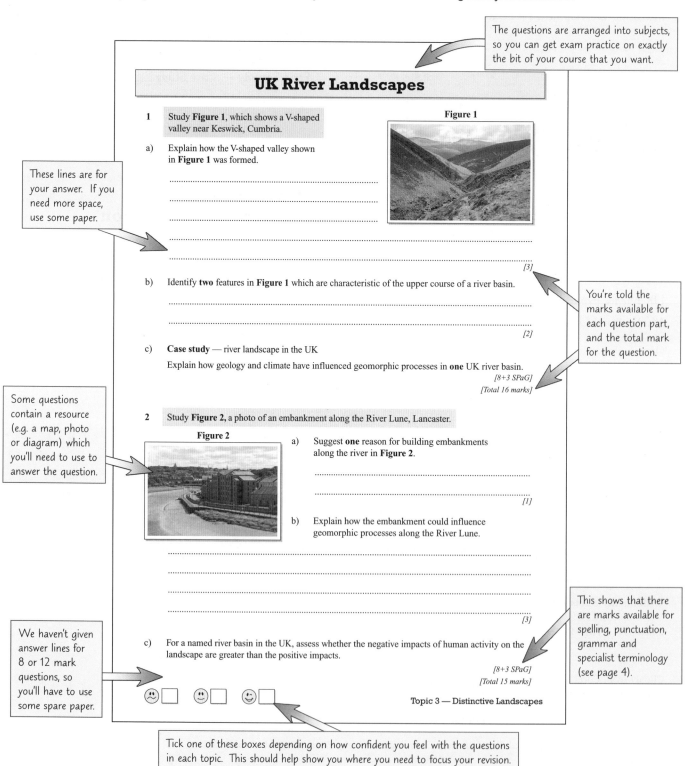

The questions are arranged into subjects, so you can get exam practice on exactly the bit of your course that you want.

UK River Landscapes

1 Study **Figure 1**, which shows a V-shaped valley near Keswick, Cumbria.

Figure 1

a) Explain how the V-shaped valley shown in **Figure 1** was formed.

....
....
....
....
....
[3]

These lines are for your answer. If you need more space, use some paper.

b) Identify **two** features in **Figure 1** which are characteristic of the upper course of a river basin.

....
....
[2]

c) **Case study** — river landscape in the UK

Explain how geology and climate have influenced geomorphic processes in **one** UK river basin.
[8+3 SPaG]
[Total 16 marks]

You're told the marks available for each question part, and the total mark for the question.

2 Study **Figure 2,** a photo of an embankment along the River Lune, Lancaster.

Figure 2

Some questions contain a resource (e.g. a map, photo or diagram) which you'll need to use to answer the question.

a) Suggest **one** reason for building embankments along the river in **Figure 2**.

....
....
[1]

b) Explain how the embankment could influence geomorphic processes along the River Lune.

....
....
....
....
[3]

This shows that there are marks available for spelling, punctuation, grammar and specialist terminology (see page 4).

c) For a named river basin in the UK, assess whether the negative impacts of human activity on the landscape are greater than the positive impacts.
[8+3 SPaG]
[Total 15 marks]

We haven't given answer lines for 8 or 12 mark questions, so you'll have to use some spare paper.

😟 ☐   🙂 ☐   😃 ☐

Topic 3 — Distinctive Landscapes

Tick one of these boxes depending on how confident you feel with the questions in each topic. This should help show you where you need to focus your revision.

Exam Breakdown

Welcome to the wonderful world of <u>exam practice</u>. This book will help you get a bit of practice at the kind of questions they're going to throw at you in the exam. It'll also help you to figure out <u>what</u> you <u>need to revise</u> — try answering the questions for the topics you've learnt in class, and if there are any questions that you <u>can't answer</u> then <u>go back and revise that topic</u> some more.

You'll have to do Three Exams

First up, here's <u>what</u> you've got to do — we'll come on to <u>how to do it</u> in a bit.

You'll have to do <u>three exams</u> — <u>one</u> on each of the <u>three components</u>. <u>Geographical skills</u> will be assessed in <u>all three</u> exams, but <u>fieldwork</u> will only be assessed in <u>Papers 1</u> and <u>2</u>.

<u>All</u> your <u>exams</u> will take place at the <u>end of the course</u>.

Paper 1: Our Natural World

Paper 1 is divided into <u>two sections</u> (A and B).

<u>Section A</u> covers <u>four topics</u>:
- Global Hazards
- Changing Climate
- Distinctive Landscapes
- Sustaining Ecosystems

<u>Section B</u> covers Physical Geography <u>Fieldwork</u>.

You have to <u>answer all the questions</u> in this paper.

1 hour 15 minutes	70 marks in total	35% of your final mark

Paper 2: People and Society

Paper 2 is divided into <u>two sections</u> (A and B).

<u>Section A</u> covers <u>four topics</u>:
- Urban Futures
- Dynamic Development
- UK in the 21st Century
- Resource Reliance

<u>Section B</u> covers Human Geography <u>Fieldwork</u>.

You have to <u>answer all the questions</u> in this paper.

1 hour 15 minutes	70 marks in total	35% of your final mark

Paper 3: Geographical Exploration

- There isn't any <u>new content</u> to learn for Paper 3 — it's all about <u>applying</u> what you <u>already know</u>.
- You'll get a <u>Resource Booklet</u> in the exam with lots of information about a specific country.
- You could be asked about anything from '<u>Our Natural World</u>' or '<u>People and Society</u>'. The questions will ask you to <u>combine</u> ideas from the <u>different topics</u>.
- There will also be a <u>decision-making exercise</u>, where you'll have to <u>use</u> the <u>sources</u> you have been given to come to a <u>conclusion</u> about a particular <u>issue</u>.

You have to <u>answer all the questions</u> in this paper.

1 hour 30 minutes	60 marks in total	30% of your final mark

There are a few other Important Things *to* Remember

1) <u>Each exam</u> will have a separate <u>Resource Booklet</u> containing sources (e.g. photos, maps, graphs and diagrams) that you will be asked to <u>use</u> to answer some of the questions.

2) In <u>each exam</u>, there will be one question which has <u>3 extra marks</u> available for <u>spelling</u>, <u>punctuation</u> and <u>grammar</u> (see p. 4). These marks are <u>included</u> in the <u>total marks</u> given for each paper.

Answering Questions

Geography exams would be <u>lovely</u> if it wasn't for those <u>inconvenient questions</u>. A nice couple of hours of <u>peace and quiet</u> to just sit and let your mind wander... Unfortunately, daydreaming about your summer holiday don't <u>butter no parsnips</u>. So here's CGP's <u>top guide</u> to tackling those pesky questions.

Make Sure you Read the Question Properly

It's dead easy to <u>misread</u> the question and spend five minutes writing about the <u>wrong thing</u>.
Four simple tips can help you <u>avoid</u> this:

1) Figure out if it's a <u>case study question</u> — most of them helpfully say <u>CASE STUDY</u> in friendly capitals at the start of the question, and each part of the question will say something like 'for a country you have studied'. If you see this, you need to include a case study or an example you've learnt about in your answer.

2) <u>Underline</u> the <u>command words</u> in the question (the ones that tell you <u>what to do</u>):

Answers to questions with 'explain' in them often include the word '<u>because</u>' (or '<u>due to</u>').

When writing about differences, '<u>whereas</u>' is a good word to use in your answers. E.g. 'ACs have a high level of development whereas LIDCs have a lower level'.

Command word	Means write about...
Describe	what it's <u>like</u>
Explain	<u>why</u> it's like that (i.e. give <u>reasons</u>)
Compare	the <u>similarities</u> AND <u>differences</u>
Discuss	give <u>both sides</u> of an argument
Suggest why	give <u>reasons</u> for
Examine	look <u>closely</u> at something
Assess or Evaluate	weigh up <u>pros</u> and <u>cons</u>, then make a <u>judgement</u> about something

If a question asks you to describe a <u>pattern</u> (e.g. from a map or graph), make sure you identify the <u>general pattern</u>, then refer to <u>specific details</u> (including any <u>anomalies</u> — things that <u>don't</u> fit the general pattern).

These are <u>tricky customers</u>, no doubt — but they're usually worth <u>lots of marks</u>, so make sure you <u>practise</u> answering them.

3) <u>Underline</u> the <u>key words</u> (the ones that tell you what it's <u>about</u>), e.g. volcanoes, tourism, migration, counter-urbanisation, debt relief.

4) If the question says '<u>using Fig. 2</u>', bloomin' well <u>make sure</u> you've talked about <u>what Figure 2 shows</u>. <u>Don't</u> just wheel out all of your <u>geographical knowledge</u> and forget all about the photo you're <u>supposed</u> to be <u>talking about</u>. <u>Re-read</u> the <u>question</u> and your <u>answer</u> when you've <u>finished</u>, just to check.

Some Questions *are* Level Marked

Questions worth <u>6 marks or more</u> with longer written answers are <u>level marked</u>, which means you need to do these <u>things</u> to get the <u>top level</u> and a <u>high mark</u>:

Questions marked with an asterisk (*) in the exam assess the quality of your reasoning and whether you've structured your answer logically.

1) <u>Read</u> the question properly and figure out a <u>structure</u> for your answer before you start. Your answer needs to be well <u>organised</u> and <u>structured</u>, and written in a <u>logical</u> way.

2) If it's a <u>case study</u> question, include plenty of <u>relevant details</u>:

- This includes things like <u>place names</u>, <u>dates</u>, <u>statistics</u>, names of <u>organisations</u> or <u>companies</u>.
- Don't forget that they need to be <u>relevant</u> though — it's no good including the exact number of people killed in a flood when the question is about the <u>causes</u> of a flood.

3) One of the questions in each paper has <u>3 extra marks</u> available for <u>spelling</u>, <u>punctuation</u>, <u>grammar</u> and <u>specialist terminology</u> (SPaG). To get <u>top marks</u> you need to:

- Make sure your <u>spelling</u>, <u>punctuation</u> and <u>grammar</u> is <u>consistently correct</u>.
- Write in a way that makes it <u>clear</u> what you mean.
- Use a <u>wide range</u> of <u>geographical terms</u> (e.g. sustainable development) <u>correctly</u>.

SPaG questions will be marked with a pencil symbol (✎) in the exam.

Global Atmospheric Circulation

1   Study **Figure 1**, a map of the world showing bands of high and low pressure and surface winds.

Figure 1

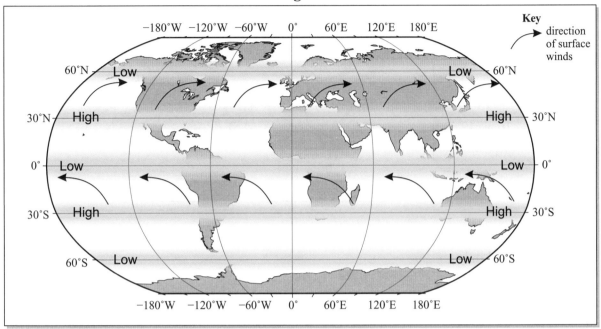

a)   Mark on **Figure 1** the direction of the surface winds between 0° and 30° N.

[1]

b)   Mark on **Figure 1** the direction of the surface winds between 60° S and 30° S.

[1]

c)   Which of the statements below best describes the movement of air at the equator?
Shade **one** oval only.

   A   Air rises up.   ⬭

   B   Air sinks down.   ⬭

   C   Air moves up and down.   ⬭

   D   Air is still and does not move.   ⬭

[1]

d)   Which of the following descriptions matches the normal weather conditions at a high pressure belt?
Shade **one** oval only.

   A   Low rainfall, often cloudy.   ⬭

   B   High rainfall, often cloudy.   ⬭

   C   Low rainfall, rarely cloudy.   ⬭

   D   High rainfall, rarely cloudy.   ⬭

[1]

[Total 4 marks]

Global Atmospheric Circulation

2   Study **Figure 2**, a map of climatic zones.

Figure 2

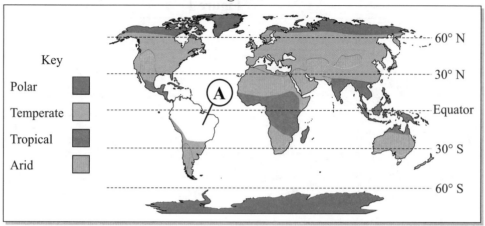

a)   **Figure 2** is incomplete. Which climatic zone is found at the location labelled A in **Figure 2**?
Shade **one** oval only.

A   Polar   ⬭

B   Temperate   ⬭

C   Tropical   ⬭

D   Arid   ⬭

[1]

b)   Explain why deserts are often found around 30° from the equator.

....

....

....

[2]

c)   Explain how global atmospheric circulation can cause extremely high temperatures
in areas of high pressure.

....

....

....

[2]

d)   Explain how global atmospheric circulation can cause extreme wind in some areas.

....

....

....

[2]

[Total 7 marks]

Extreme Weather

1   Study **Figure 1**, which gives information about the weather conditions in
a town in southern England during the first two weeks of December 2010.

Figure 1

		December 2010													
Day		1	2	3	4	5	6	7	8	9	10	11	12	13	14
Minimum temperature (°C)		−5	−3	−4	0	−1	1	−1	−2	−1	0	−2	−3	1	0
Maximum temperature (°C)		−2	1	−1	2	1	2	3	0	1	2	0	0	2	3
Precipitation (mm)		0	0	1	2	3	3	7	0	0	0	2	1	1	8

a)   Calculate the range of minimum temperatures shown in **Figure 1**.

....
[1]

b)   Calculate the mean daily precipitation during the time period shown in **Figure 1**.

....
[1]

c)   What type of extreme weather event is shown in **Figure 1**? Shade **one** oval only.

A   Tropical storm   ⬭

B   Cold snap   ⬭

C   Extremely high precipitation   ⬭

D   Heatwave   ⬭

[1]

d)   Compare extremes of temperature, precipitation and wind in contrasting countries
that you have studied.

....

....

....

....

....

....

....

....

....
[6]

[Total 9 marks]

Topic 1 — Global Hazards

8

Tropical Storms

1 Study **Figure 1**, a map showing the areas affected by tropical storms.

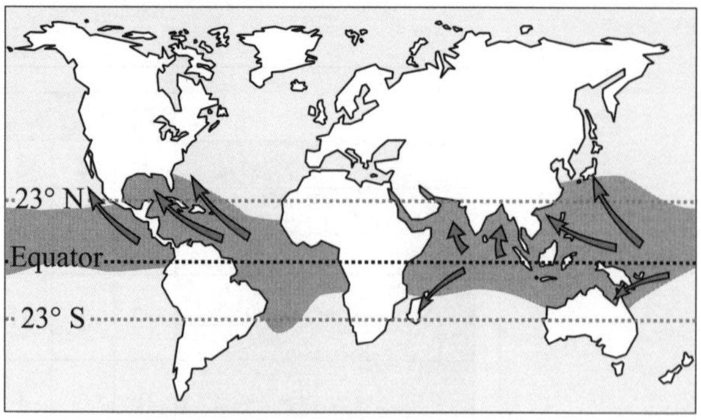

a) Using **Figure 1**, describe the global distribution of tropical storms.

Figure 1

....

....

....

....

....

....
[2]

Key

↖ path of tropical storm

● sea surface temperature 27 °C or higher

b) Explain why tropical storms are only found in the areas shown in **Figure 1**.

....

....

....
[2]

c) Which statement below best describes how the frequency and distribution of tropical storms have changed over time? Shade **one** oval only.

A The distribution stays the same, but the frequency varies from year to year. ◯

B The distribution varies, but the frequency stays roughly the same each year. ◯

C The distribution stays the same, but the frequency decreases each year. ◯

D The distribution and the frequency stay exactly the same each year. ◯
[1]

d) Describe the extreme weather conditions associated with tropical storms and explain how they are caused.

....

....

....

....

....

....

....
[6]

[Total 11 marks]

El Niño and La Niña

1   **Figure 1** shows normal atmospheric and oceanic circulation patterns in the South Pacific Ocean.

Figure 1

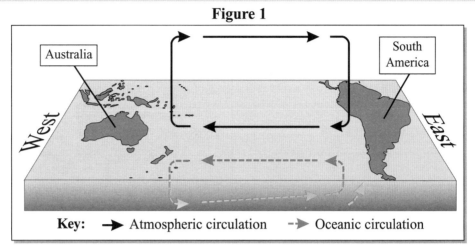

Key: → Atmospheric circulation   ⇢ Oceanic circulation

a)   Describe how the circulation patterns shown in **Figure 1** change during an El Niño event.

....

....

....

....

....

....

[4]

b)   Explain how El Niño events can cause droughts in some areas.

....

....

....

[2]

c)   Describe how the circulation patterns shown in **Figure 1** change during a La Niña event.

....

....

....

[2]

d)   Outline the extreme weather that may be experienced on the west coast of South America during a La Niña event.

....

....

[1]

[Total 9 marks]

Topic 1 — Global Hazards

Drought

1 Study **Figure 1**, which shows the global distribution of areas affected by drought in November 2008.

Figure 1

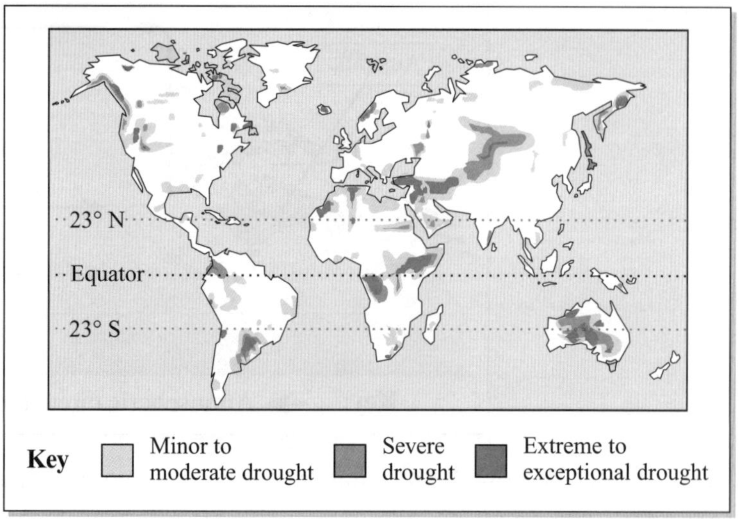

a) Describe the global distribution of areas affected by extreme to exceptional drought.

Refer to named regions or countries in your answer.

....

....

....

....

....

....

....

....

....

[4]

Key

☐ Minor to moderate drought   ☐ Severe drought   ■ Extreme to exceptional drought

(map showing 23° N, Equator, 23° S)

b) Describe what a drought is.

....

....

[1]

c) Which statement below best describes how the distribution of droughts has changed over time? Shade **one** oval only.

   A   The distribution of droughts has not changed much.   ⬭

   B   There have been more droughts in the Americas and Russia since 1950.   ⬭

   C   There have been more droughts in Africa and Asia since 1950.   ⬭

   D   There have been fewer droughts in Africa and Asia since 1950.   ⬭

   [1]

d) Describe how the frequency of droughts has changed over time, and suggest how it might change in the future.

   ....

   ....

   ....

   [2]

   [Total 8 marks]

Extreme Weather — Case Studies

Answer Questions 1 and 2 using case studies of extreme weather events.
Use **one** UK-based case study and **one** non-UK-based case study.

1   Answer this question using a case study of **either** a tropical storm **or** a flash flooding event.

Chosen weather hazard event:...

a)   Explain how specific factors, including extreme weather conditions,
      caused the weather hazard event.

   ....

   ....

   ....

   ....

   ....
                                                                                                          [4]

b)   Describe the consequences of the weather hazard event.

   ....

   ....

   ....

   ....

   ....
                                                                                                          [4]

c)   Describe how people and organisations responded to the weather hazard event.

   ....

   ....

   ....

   ....

   ....
                                                                                                          [4]
                                                                                              [Total 12 marks]

2   Answer this question using a case study of **either** a drought **or** a heat wave event.

Chosen weather hazard event:...

Outline the consequences of this weather hazard event and the responses to it.

                                                                                              [Total 8 + 3 SPaG]

Tectonic Plates

1   Study **Figure 1**, a diagram showing the Earth's structure.

Figure 1

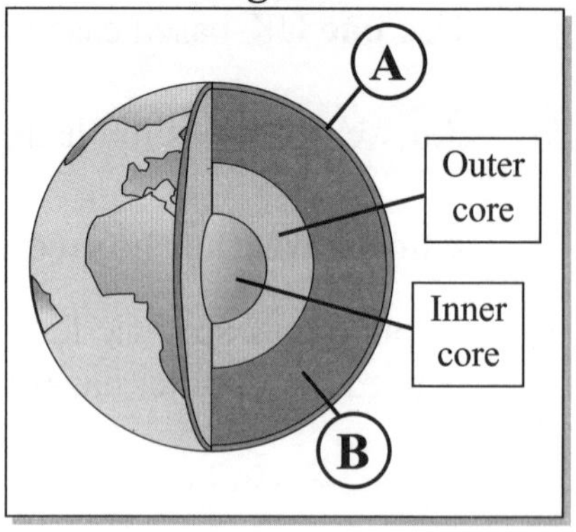

a)   What feature is labelled A in **Figure 1**? Shade **one** oval only.

    A   Crust ⬭

    B   Plate boundary ⬭

    C   Mantle ⬭

    D   Magma ⬭

[1]

b)   Name and describe the feature labelled B in **Figure 1**.

....

....

....

[2]

c)   Which statement below best describes the difference between the inner core and the outer core?
Shade **one** oval only.

    A   The inner core is liquid; the outer core is solid. ⬭

    B   The inner core is solid; the outer core is liquid. ⬭

    C   The outer core is divided into tectonic plates; the inner core is not. ⬭

    D   The inner core is divided into tectonic plates; the outer core is not. ⬭

[1]

d)   Describe how continental crust is different from oceanic crust.

....

....

....

[2]

e)   Explain how convection currents cause tectonic plates to move.

....

....

....

....

....

....

[4]

[Total 10 marks]

Plate Boundaries

1 Study **Figure 1**, which shows the Earth's tectonic plates.

Figure 1

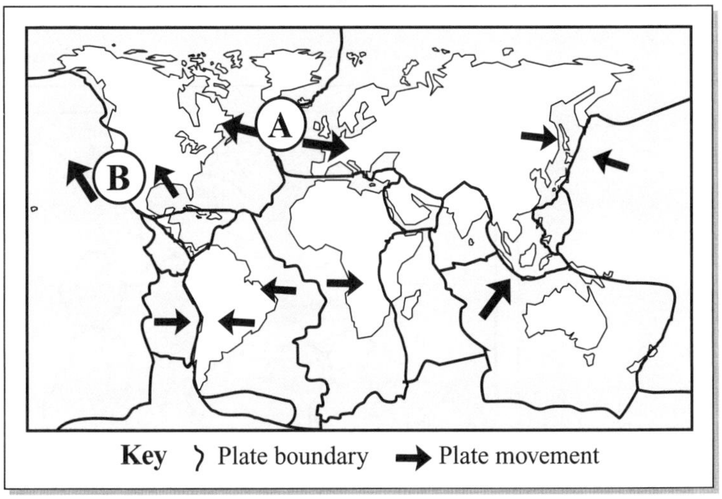

a) Name the type of plate boundary labelled A in **Figure 1** and explain why new crust forms there.

....

....

....

....

....

....

....

[3]

b) Name the type of plate boundary found at the location labelled B on **Figure 1**.

....

[1]

c) Describe **two** ways that tectonic plates could move in relation to each other at the type of plate boundary you identified in b).

....

....

....

[2]

d) Study **Figure 2**, which is a diagram of a plate boundary. Name the type of plate boundary shown.

....

[1]

Figure 2

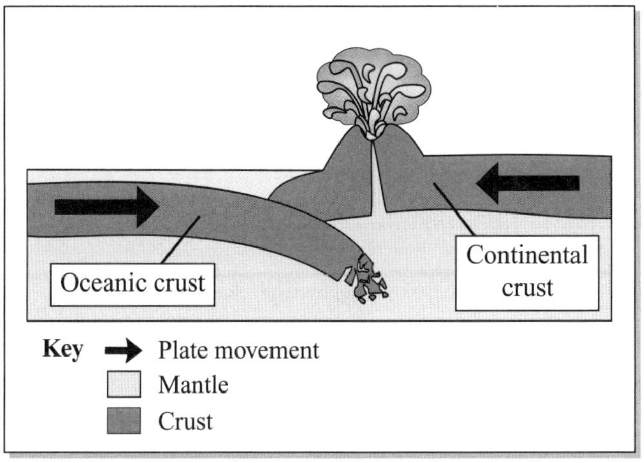

Oceanic crust

Continental crust

Key ➡ Plate movement
☐ Mantle
☐ Crust

e) Describe the processes that operate at a collision plate boundary.

....

....

....

....

....

....

[2]

[Total 9 marks]

Tectonic Hazards

1   Study **Figure 1**, which shows the Earth's tectonic plates and the distribution of earthquakes.

Figure 1

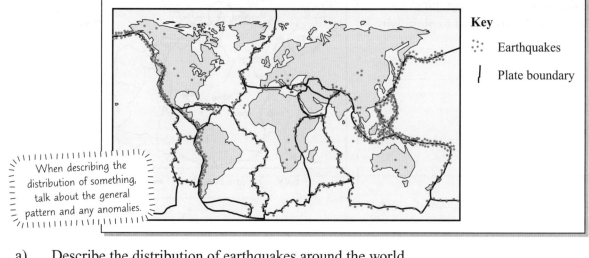

When describing the distribution of something, talk about the general pattern and any anomalies.

Key

∴ Earthquakes

| Plate boundary

a)   Describe the distribution of earthquakes around the world.

....

....

....
[2]

b)   Explain how earthquakes are caused at destructive plate boundaries.

....

....

....

....

....
[3]

c)   Describe what a shallow-focus earthquake is.

....

....
[1]

d)   Explain the causes of deep-focus earthquakes.

....

....

....

....
[2]

[Total 8 marks]

Tectonic Hazards

2 Study **Figure 2**, which shows the Earth's tectonic plates and the distribution of volcanoes.

a) Describe the global distribution of volcanoes.

....

....

....

....

....

....

[2]

Figure 2

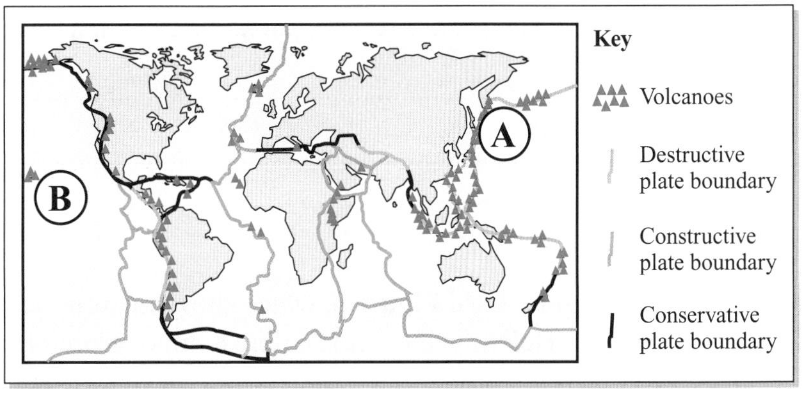

Key

▲▲▲ Volcanoes

Destructive plate boundary

Constructive plate boundary

Conservative plate boundary

b) Name the type of plate boundary labelled A in **Figure 2** and explain how volcanoes are formed at this location.

....

....

....

....

....

[4]

c) Hawaii is labelled B on **Figure 2**. There are volcanoes in Hawaii, even though it is in the centre of a tectonic plate. Explain how volcanoes form away from plate boundaries.

....

....

....

....

[3]

[Total 9 marks]

3 Study **Figure 3**, which shows a cross-section through a shield volcano.

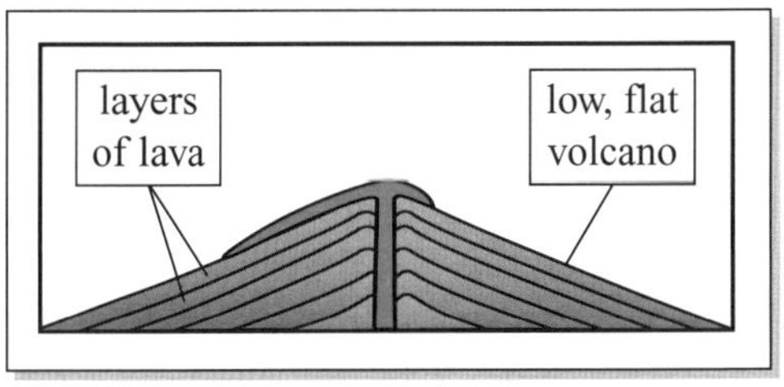

a) Explain how the volcano gets its characteristic shape.

Figure 3

layers of lava

low, flat volcano

....

....

....

....

[2]

Tectonic Hazards

b) Contrast the characteristics of shield volcanoes and composite volcanoes.

'Contrast' means write about the differences.

....

....

....

....

[4]

[Total 6 marks]

4 Study **Figure 4** and **Figure 5**, which show measurements made by scientists on Mount St. Helens in the USA, before a minor eruption on the 19th March 1982.

Draw your own lines on graphs in the exam to help you read them.

Figure 4

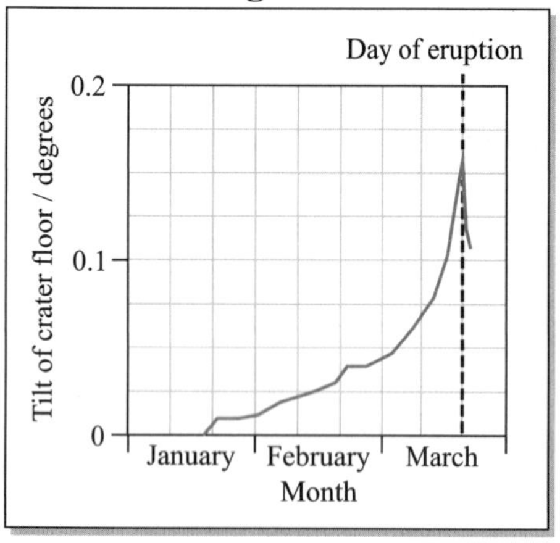

Figure 5

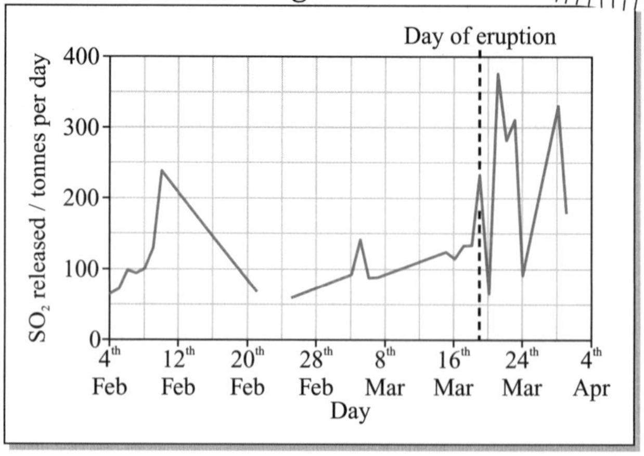

a) Suggest why the crater floor bulged up before the volcano erupted, causing the increased tilt shown in **Figure 4**.

....

....

[1]

b) How much sulfur dioxide was released on the day of the eruption?

....

[1]

c) Complete **Figure 5** to show that 100 tonnes of sulfur dioxide were released on 24th February.

[1]

d) Which measurement (the tilt of the crater floor or the release of sulfur dioxide) gave a better warning of when the volcano was going to erupt? Explain your answer.

....

....

....

[3]

e) For a tectonic hazard event that you have studied, examine the consequences of the event and the responses to it.

[8 + 3 SPaG]

[Total 17 marks]

Managing the Impacts of Tectonic Hazards

1   **Figure 1** shows Yokohama, a city in Japan. Yokohama is close to Mount Fuji, an active volcano. The area is also prone to earthquakes.

Figure 1

a)   Explain how buildings and other structures in Yokohama might have been designed to reduce the effects of earthquakes **or** volcanic eruptions.

....

....

....

....

....
                                                                                                                              [4]

b)   Other than building design, explain how technological developments can help to reduce the effects of **either** volcanoes **or** earthquakes in areas at risk from tectonic hazards.

....

....

....

....

....

....

....

....

....
                                                                                                                              [6]
                                                                                                        [Total 10 marks]

Climate Change — Evidence and Causes

1   Study **Figure 1**, a graph showing temperature changes during the Quaternary period.

a)   Describe the general trends shown in **Figure 1**.

....

....

....

....

....

....

....

                                                                       [2]

Figure 1

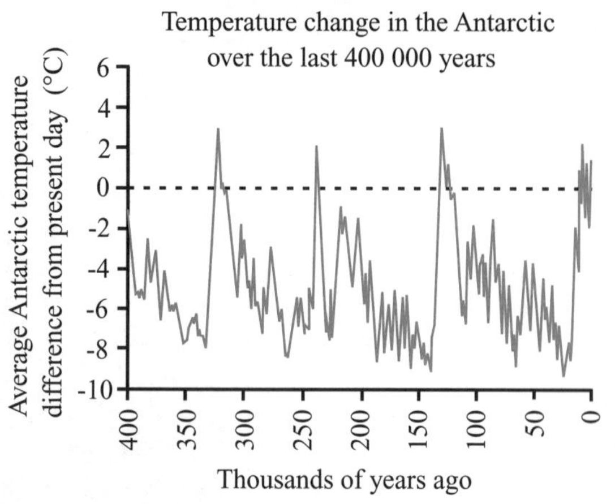

Temperature change in the Antarctic over the last 400 000 years

b)   The temperature changes shown in **Figure 1** were worked out from ice core records.
Explain how ice cores provide evidence for past climate change.

....

....

....

                                                                                                           [2]

c)   Outline **one** other source of evidence for long-term climate change and briefly evaluate its reliability.

....

....

....

....

....

                                                                                                           [3]

d)   Explain **two** possible causes of the changes in temperature between
400 000 and 100 000 years ago shown in **Figure 1**.

1:..

....

....

2:..

....

                                                                                                           [4]

                                                                                                        [Total 11 marks]

Climate Change — Evidence and Causes

2 Study **Figure 2**, which shows global temperature between 1860 and 2000.

a) How much did global temperature rise by between 1860 and 2000?

....
[1]

Figure 2

b) Describe the change in average global temperature shown by the graph.

....

....

....

....

....

....
[2]

[Total 3 marks]

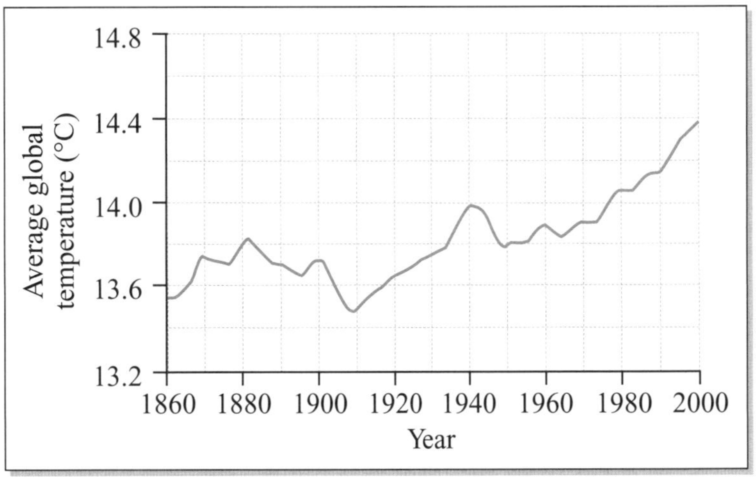

3 Study **Figure 3**, a photograph of a coal-fired power plant in South Africa.

a) Explain what impact this activity may have on climate change.

Figure 3

....

....

....

....

....

....

....

....

....
[4]

b) Outline **one** other human activity that may contribute to climate change.

....

....

....
[2]

[Total 6 marks]

Global Effects of Climate Change

1 Study **Figure 1**, which shows data on sea level rise between 1900 and 2100.

Figure 1

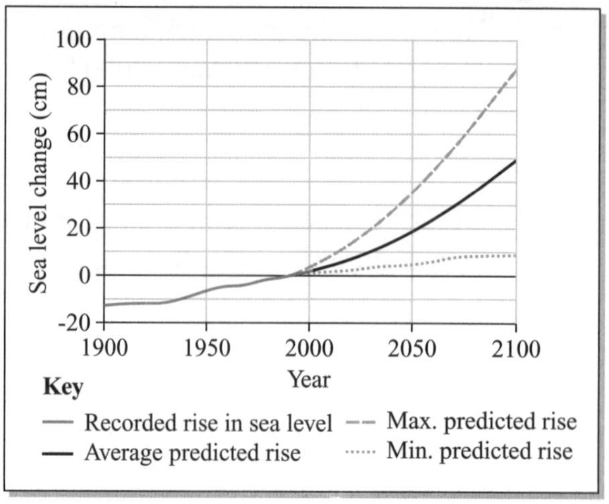

a) What is the average predicted rise in sea level between 2050 and 2100?

....
[1]

b) Suggest **one** way in which the rise in sea level might affect the environment.

....

....

....
[1]

Key
— Recorded rise in sea level -- Max. predicted rise
— Average predicted rise ······ Min. predicted rise

c) Apart from sea level rise, outline **two** possible environmental impacts of climate change.

1:...

....

2:...

....
[2]

[Total 4 marks]

2 Study **Figure 2**, which shows the maize yield and annual rainfall for a low latitude farm in Central Africa.

Figure 2

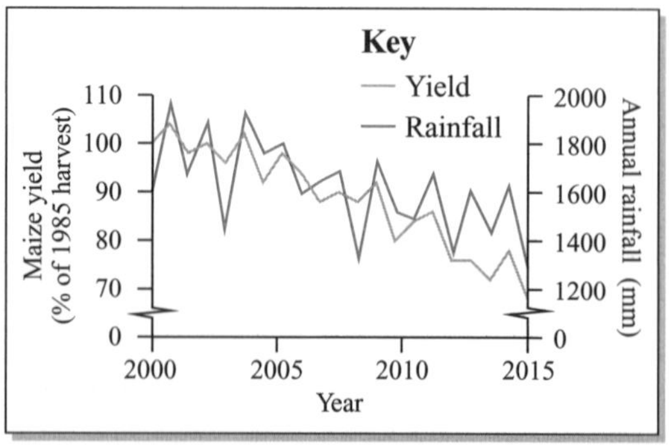

a) Using **Figure 2**, describe how climate change may be affecting crop yields in low latitude areas.

....

....

....

....
[2]

b) Suggest **one** possible social impact of the trends in crop yield shown in **Figure 2**.

....

....
[1]

c) Outline **one** economic impact, other than changing crop yields, that climate change may cause.

....

....
[1]

[Total 4 marks]

Topic 2 — Changing Climate

Effects of Climate Change on the UK

1   Study **Figure 1**, a newspaper article about tourism in the UK.

Figure 1

Bank Holiday Weekend Tourist Boom

Thousands of tourists flocked to the South West's beaches over the bank holiday weekend to enjoy unusually warm temperatures.

In some areas there were highs of 32 °C, which attracted thousands of beachgoers and holiday-makers.

It's thought the good weather has encouraged many UK residents to take a 'staycation' instead of travelling abroad to continental destinations.

This is good news for the South West's tourism industry. Tourists contribute an average of £4 billion every year to the local economy — an important source of income for the region.

a)   Suggest why the weather described in **Figure 1** may become more common in the UK.

....

....

....

[2]

b)   Using **Figure 1** and your own knowledge, describe the positive impacts that climate change may have on the UK.

....

....

....

....

....

[3]

c)   Outline **two** possible social impacts of climate change in the UK.

1:...

....

....

2:...

....

....

[4]

d)   Assess whether the negative environmental impacts of climate change in the UK in the 21st century are likely to be more significant than the negative economic impacts.

[8 + 3 SPaG]

[Total 20 marks]

Topic 2 — Changing Climate

The UK Landscape

1   Study **Figure 1**, a map of the UK's upland and lowland areas.

Figure 1

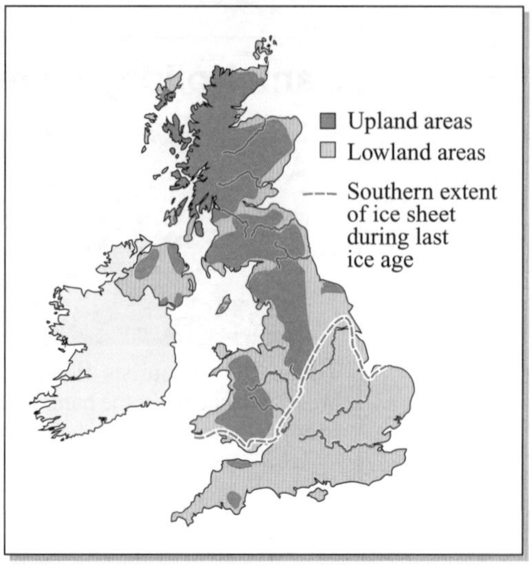

a)   Describe the distribution of upland landscapes in the UK.

....

....

....

....

....

....

[2]

b)   Which of the following is true of the climate of upland landscapes? Shade **one** oval only.

    A   Temperatures are high.   ⬭

    B   Snow is very uncommon.   ⬭

    C   Rainfall is relatively high.   ⬭

    D   Rainfall is relatively low.   ⬭

[1]

c)   Outline the physical characteristics of lowland areas in the UK.

....

....

....

[2]

d)   Compare land uses in upland and lowland areas in the UK.

....

....

....

....

....

....

[4]

e)   Briefly describe what is meant by a natural landscape.

....

....

[1]

[Total 10 marks]

Weathering and Erosion

1 Study **Figure 1**, which shows how the coastline of an area has changed over time.

Figure 1

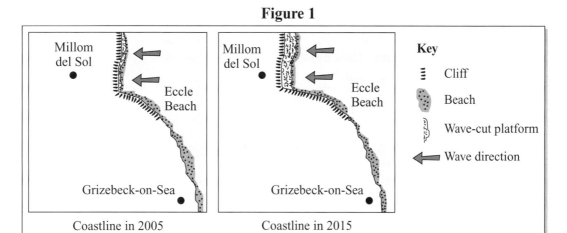

a) Name and describe **two** processes of erosion that could have caused the coastal change shown in **Figure 1**.

It's a four mark question, so there are two marks for each process.

1:..

....

....

2:..

....

....

[4]

b) Explain how freeze-thaw weathering could cause the cliffs shown in **Figure 1** to break up.

....

....

....

....

....

....

[4]

c) Describe a process of weathering, other than freeze-thaw, that can affect landscapes.

....

....

....

[2]

[Total 10 marks]

Topic 3 — Distinctive Landscapes

Transportation and Deposition

1 Study **Figure 1**, which shows how the velocity of the River Dance varies along its course.

a) Small gravel particles are transported by velocities above 0.1 m per second.
At what distance along the River Dance does the transportation of gravel start?

....
[1]

Figure 1

b) At 80 km along the River Dance, pebbles are being transported.
Give the velocity of the river at this point.

....
[1]

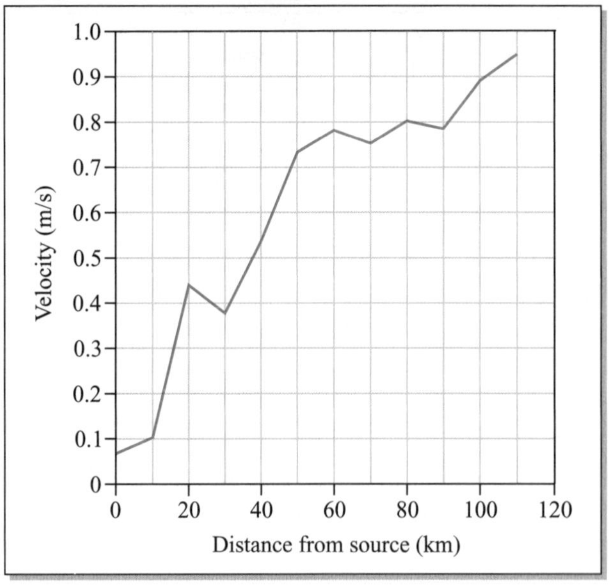

c) Using **Figure 1**, suggest why deposition is the dominant process between 20 and 30 km.

....

....

....
[2]

d) In the tables below, match each process of transportation with its correct description.
One has been done for you.

Process of transportation
Saltation
Solution
Traction
Suspension

Description
Large particles like boulders are pushed along the river bed or sea floor by the force of the water.
Soluble materials dissolve in the water and are carried along.
Small particles like silt and clay are carried along by the water.
Pebble-sized particles are bounced along the river bed or sea floor by the force of the water.

[2]

e) Explain how constructive waves contribute to deposition on the coast.

....

....

....

....
[3]

[Total 9 marks]

Topic 3 — Distinctive Landscapes

Coastal Landforms

1 Study **Figure 1**, a photograph showing coastal landforms.

a) Name the type of landform labelled A in **Figure 1**.

....
[1]

b) Explain how the landforms shown in **Figure 1** are formed.

Figure 1

....
....
....
....
....
....
....
[3]
[Total 4 marks]

2 Study **Figure 2**, a photograph of a coastal area.

Use evidence from **Figure 2** to suggest how this coastal area may change in the future. Explain your answer.

Figure 2

....
....
....
....
....
....
....
....
....
For this question you have to describe what the area will look like and explain why.
....
....
[Total 4 marks]

Topic 3 — Distinctive Landscapes

Coastal Landforms

3 Study **Figure 3**, an Ordnance Survey® map of a coastal area in Devon.

Figure 3

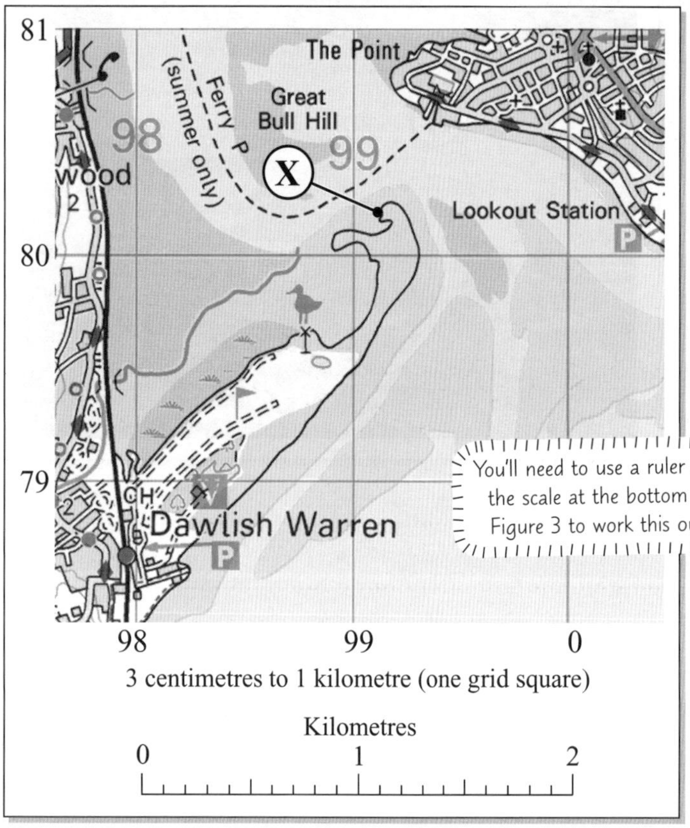

3 centimetres to 1 kilometre (one grid square)

Kilometres

You'll need to use a ruler and the scale at the bottom of Figure 3 to work this out.

a) What is the six-figure grid reference for the end of the spit, marked X on **Figure 3**? Shade **one** oval only.

A   992818   ⬭

B   991802   ⬭

C   090818   ⬭

D   802991   ⬭

[1]

b) What is the distance between the end of the spit and Dawlish Warren station at 979786?

.... km

[1]

c) Explain how the spit shown in **Figure 3** was formed.

....

....

....

....

[3]

d) Describe the erosional landforms in **one** coastal landscape you have studied, and explain how they were formed.

Name of coastal landscape: ....

....

....

....

....

....

....

....

....

....

....

[6]

[Total 11 marks]

Topic 3 — Distinctive Landscapes

UK Coastal Landscapes

1   Study **Figure 1**, a photo of erosion on the Holderness Coast.

a)   Describe how geology may be influencing erosion
on the stretch of coast shown in **Figure 1**.

Figure 1

....

....

....

....

....

....

....

[3]

b)   Using **Figure 1** and your own knowledge, suggest how the process of erosion could be managed
to help protect the Holderness coast.

....

....

....

....

....

[4]

[Total 7 marks]

2   Study **Figure 2**, a photo of a stretch of the South West Coast Path in Cornwall.

Figure 2

a)   Describe how human activity has affected the
clifftop in **Figure 2**.

....

....

....

....

....

....

[2]

b)   **Case study** — coastal landscape in the UK

Assess how far the impacts of human activity on **one** coastal landscape have been negative.

[8+3 SPaG]

[Total 13 marks]

River Landforms

1   Study **Figure 1**, which shows a drainage basin.

Figure 1

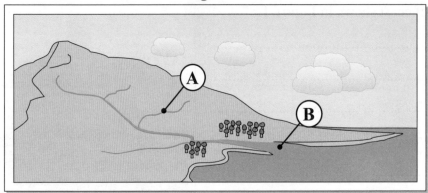

a)   Identify the feature labelled A in **Figure 1**. Shade **one** oval only.

   A   Tributary   ○

   B   Confluence   ○

   C   Floodplain   ○

   D   Lower course   ○   *[1]*

b)   Identify the feature labelled B in **Figure 1**.

   ....
                                                                                 [1]
                                                                        [Total 2 marks]

2   Study **Figure 2**, a cross profile of a river.   **Figure 2**

a)   Draw lines to match the labels Y and Z to the
     correct river feature.

   [Y]   [Floodplain]

   [Z]   [Levee]

              [Estuary]   *[2]*

b)   Where in a river basin would you expect to find the features in **Figure 2**?

   ....
                                                                                 [1]

c)   Explain how the landform labelled Y in **Figure 2** is formed.

   ....

   ....

   ....

   ....
                                                                                 [3]
                                                                        [Total 6 marks]

River Landforms

3   Study **Figure 3**, which is an Ordnance Survey® map showing part of Snowdonia, Wales.

Figure 3

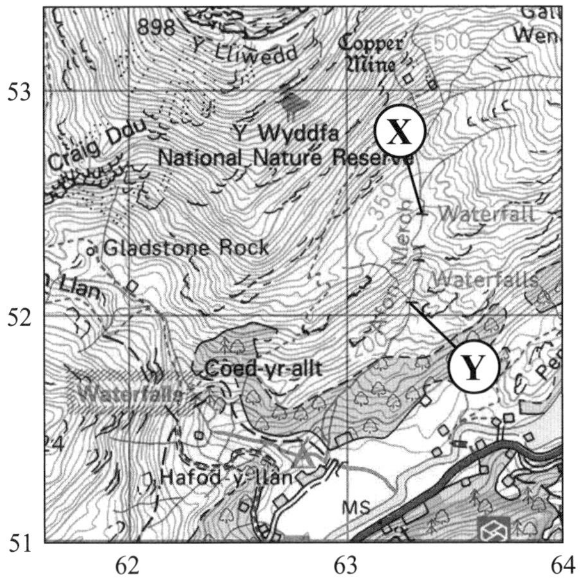

3 centimetres to 1 kilometre (one grid square)

Kilometres
0   1   2

a)   What is the six-figure grid reference for the waterfall, marked X on **Figure 3**? Shade **one** oval only.

A   525634   ⬭

B   647535   ⬭

C   633524   ⬭

D   635535   ⬭

[1]

b)   There is another waterfall at point Y. State the distance between the two waterfalls.

....
[1]

c)   Which waterfall, X or Y, is located on a steeper section of the river's course?

....
[1]

d)   Suggest why waterfalls have formed along this stretch of the Afon Merch.

....

....

....
[2]

e)   Explain how a gorge may form in the upper course of the Afon Merch.

....

....

....

....

....
[3]

f)   Geographical Information Systems (GIS) are able to show a range of types of geographical data on separate layers. Suggest **one** layer that could be added to **Figure 3** to help understand the formation of river landforms.

....

....
[1]

[Total 9 marks]

River Landforms

4 Study **Figure 4**, which is a labelled photograph of a meander.

a) Suggest a feature likely to be found at the part of the river labelled A in **Figure 4** and explain its formation.

....

....

....

....

....

....

[3]

Figure 4

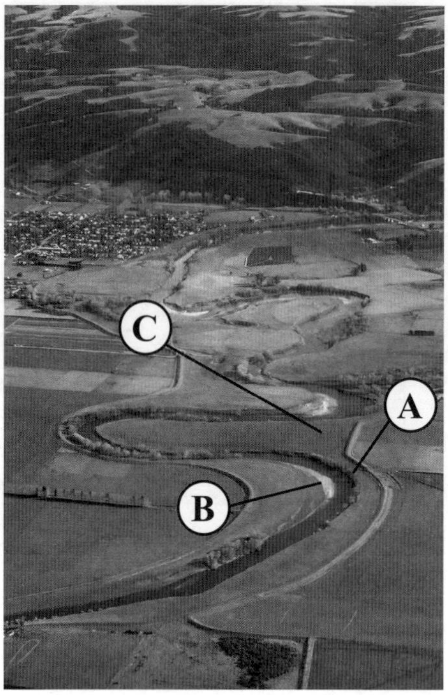

b) Suggest a feature likely to be found at the part of the river labelled B in **Figure 4** and explain its formation.

....

....

....

....

....

....

[3]

c) Name the feature labelled C in **Figure 4**.

....

[1]

d) Explain how an ox-bow lake could form on the river shown in **Figure 4**.

....

....

....

....

....

....

....

[6]

[Total 13 marks]

Topic 3 — Distinctive Landscapes

UK River Landscapes

1 Study **Figure 1**, which shows a V-shaped valley near Keswick, Cumbria.

Figure 1

a) Explain how the V-shaped valley shown in **Figure 1** was formed.

....

....

....

....

....

[3]

b) Identify **two** features in **Figure 1** which are characteristic of the upper course of a river basin.

....

....

[2]

c) **Case study** — river landscape in the UK

Explain how geology and climate have influenced geomorphic processes in **one** UK river basin.

[8+3 SPaG]

[Total 16 marks]

2 Study **Figure 2,** a photo of an embankment along the River Lune, Lancaster.

Figure 2

a) Suggest **one** reason for building embankments along the river in **Figure 2**.

....

....

[1]

b) Explain how the embankment could influence geomorphic processes along the River Lune.

....

....

....

....

[3]

c) For a named river basin in the UK, assess whether the negative impacts of human activity on the landscape are greater than the positive impacts.

[8+3 SPaG]

[Total 15 marks]

Topic 3 — Distinctive Landscapes

Ecosystems

1 Study **Figure 1**, which shows part of a food web for a coastal ecosystem.

a) Using **Figure 1**, describe how the sea snail and the periwinkle are connected to each other.

....

....

....

....
[1]

Figure 1

Figure 1 shows a food web with the following organisms: Sea urchin, Sea otter, Seaweed, Crab, Octopus, Sea snail, Periwinkle.

b) Give **one** non-living component that could be part of this ecosystem.

....
[1]

c) Using **Figure 1**, explain how the populations of octopuses and seaweed in this ecosystem might be affected if a disease reduced the crab population.

Octopuses: ....

....

Seaweed: ....

....
[2]

d) Using **Figure 1**, explain how the organisms in the food web might be affected if more sea otters were introduced into the area.

....

....

....

....
[3]

e) Describe **one** way that soil and plants are dependent on one another in land-based ecosystems.

....

....

....
[2]

[Total 9 marks]

Global Ecosystems

1 Study **Figure 1**, a map showing the distribution of some of the world's ecosystems.

Figure 1

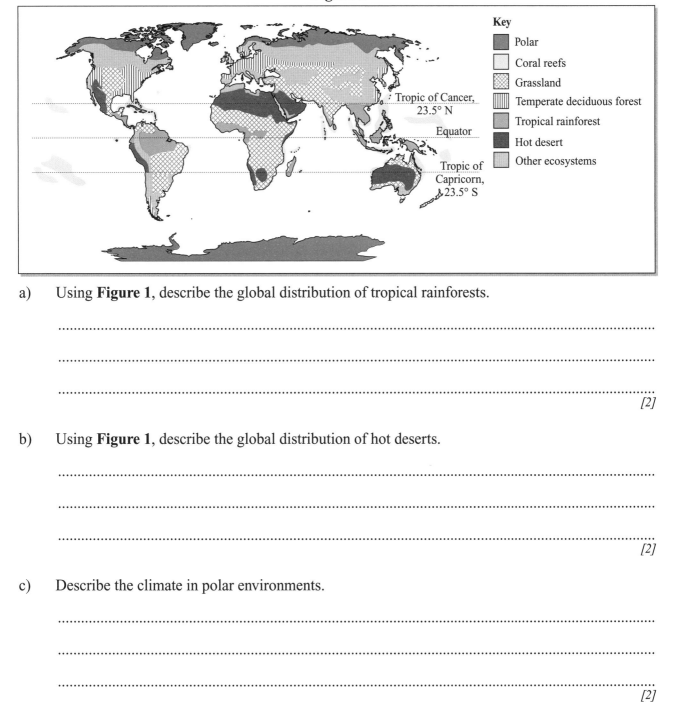

a) Using **Figure 1**, describe the global distribution of tropical rainforests.

....

....

....
[2]

b) Using **Figure 1**, describe the global distribution of hot deserts.

....

....

....
[2]

c) Describe the climate in polar environments.

....

....

....
[2]

d) Which statement best describes the characteristics of the vegetation of polar ecosystems?
Shade **one** oval only.

A The vegetation is evergreen because the climate is cold all year round.   ⬭

B The trees drop their leaves in the winter to cope with the colder weather.   ⬭

C The vegetation is dense because winters are long.   ⬭

D The vegetation is stunted because the growing season is very short.   ⬭
[1]

[Total 7 marks]

Topic 4 — Sustaining Ecosystems

Global Ecosystems

2   Study **Figure 2**, which shows climate data for a hot desert.

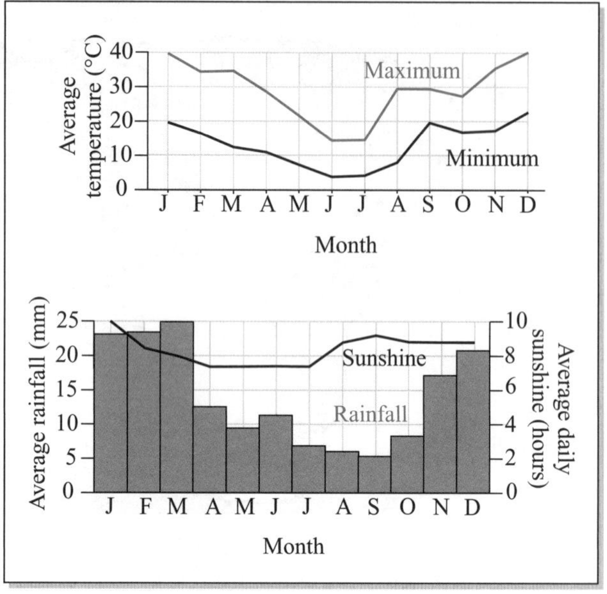

a)   What is the average maximum temperature for December?

.... °C

[1]

Figure 2

b)   With reference to **Figure 2**, describe **two** characteristics of the hot desert climate.

Characteristic 1: ....

....

....

....

Characteristic 2: ....

....

[4]

c)   Outline the typical characteristics of plants in hot deserts.

....

....

....

....

....

[3]

[Total 8 marks]

Figure 3

Diet: Plants
Length: 5-15 cm
Behaviour: Nocturnal. Live in burrows.

3   Study **Figure 3**, a mini fact file about the desert jerboa.

Using **Figure 3** and your own knowledge, explain **two** ways in which jerboas are characteristic of the animals found in the hot deserts.

1:...

....

2:...

....

[Total 4 marks]

Global Ecosystems

4 Study **Figure 4**, a photograph of savannah grassland.

a) Where are grasslands found?

....

.... *[1]*

Figure 4

b) Which of the following is **not** a characteristic of the climate of grasslands? Shade **one** oval only.

A   Cold winters (down to –40 °C)   ⬭

B   Distinct wet and dry seasons   ⬭

C   High rainfall (over 1500 mm/yr)   ⬭

D   Hot summers (up to 40 °C)   ⬭   *[1]*

c) Using **Figure 4** and your own knowledge, describe the flora of grassland ecosystems.

....

....

....
[2]

[Total 4 marks]

5 Coral reefs are found between 30° north and south of the equator, close to the coast.

a) Explain why coral reefs are found in this location.

....

....

....

....

....
[3]

b) Describe how coral and algae form an interconnected relationship in coral reefs.

....

....

....
[2]

[Total 5 marks]

Global Ecosystems

6   Study **Figure 5**, which shows temperature and rainfall data for an area of temperate forest.

Figure 5

Month	Average temperature / °C	Average rainfall / mm
January	2	64
February	5	42
March	6	33
April	12	42
May	19	45
June	19	48
July	21	69
August	19	62
September	12	45
October	10	55
November	4	65
December	2	52

a)   Which month has the highest average temperature?

....

[1]

b)   Use **Figure 5** to describe the climate of this temperate forest.

....

....

....

....

....

....

[2]

c)   Briefly describe the global distribution of temperate forests.

....

....

....

[1]

d)   Which of the following animal species is most likely to be found in a temperate forest? Shade **one** oval only.

      A   Zebra   ◯

      B   Fox   ◯

      C   Camel   ◯

      D   Polar bear   ◯

[1]

e)   Describe the flora found in temperate forests.

....

....

....

....

....

[4]

[Total 9 marks]

Topic 4 — Sustaining Ecosystems

Tropical Rainforests

1   Study **Figure 1**, a photograph of an area of tropical rainforest in Myanmar.

a)   Using **Figure 1**, outline **two** characteristics of the vegetation in tropical rainforests.

Figure 1

Characteristic 1: ....

....

....

....

Characteristic 2: ....

....

....

[2]

b)   Describe the climate of tropical rainforests.

....

....

....

....

[3]

c)   Which of the following is **not** a common characteristic of the fauna of tropical rainforests? Shade **one** oval only.

   A   Nocturnal   ◯

   B   Camouflaged   ◯

   C   Thick layer of blubber   ◯

   D   Excellent sense of smell ◯

[1]

d)   Describe the interdependence between flora and fauna in tropical rainforest ecosystems.

....

....

....

....

[2]

[Total 8 marks]

Tropical Rainforests

2 Study **Figure 2**, a diagram showing part of the water cycle in tropical rainforests.

a) Name the processes labelled A and B in **Figure 2**.

A:...

B:...

[2]

Figure 2

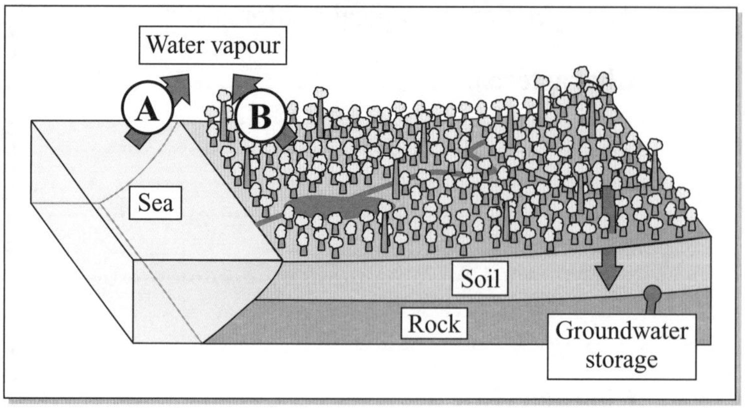

b) Explain why rainfall levels are high in tropical rainforests.

....

....

....

....

[2]

c) Explain how the density of vegetation in tropical rainforests affects the water cycle.

....

....

....

[2]

[Total 6 marks]

3 Study **Figure 3**, a diagram showing part of the nutrient cycle in a tropical rainforest ecosystem.

a) State how nutrients are transferred along the arrow labelled A in **Figure 3**.

....

....

[1]

Figure 3

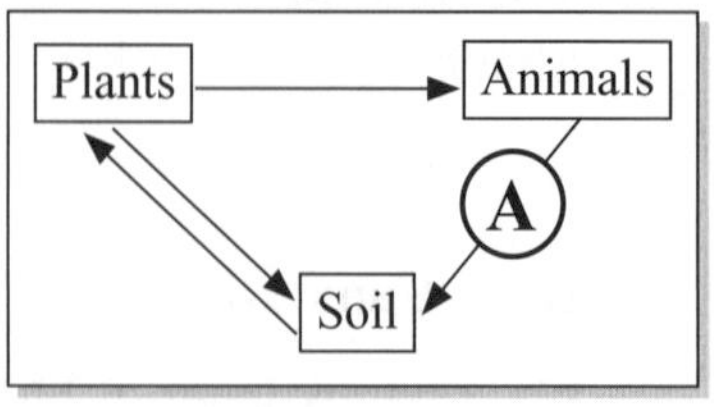

b) Describe how nutrients are recycled in the rest of the tropical rainforest ecosystem in **Figure 3**.

....

....

....

....

....

....

[4]

[Total 5 marks]

Tropical Rainforests

4 Study **Figure 4**, a photograph showing exposed soil in an area of tropical rainforest.

Figure 4

a) Which statement best describes the soil profile of rainforest soils? Shade **one** oval only.

A Rainforest soils are shallow and infertile. ◯

B There is a thick leaf layer but the nutrient-rich layer is thin. ◯

C Rainforest soils are shallow with a thin layer of humus. ◯

D The deep soils are fertile, with a thick leaf layer. ◯

[1]

b) Explain how the climate affects the characteristics of the soils that form in tropical rainforests.

....

....

....

....

....

[4]

[Total 5 marks]

5 Study **Figure 5**, a diagram of an epiphyte in a tropical rainforest. Epiphytes are plants that grow on other plants, but which do not obtain nutrients from their hosts.

a) State **one** possible reason why epiphytes grow high up in the canopy.

....

....

[1]

Figure 5

Rainfall

Epiphyte

Tree

b) Using **Figure 5** and your own knowledge, suggest how epiphytes are dependent on other parts of the ecosystem.

....

....

....

....

....

....

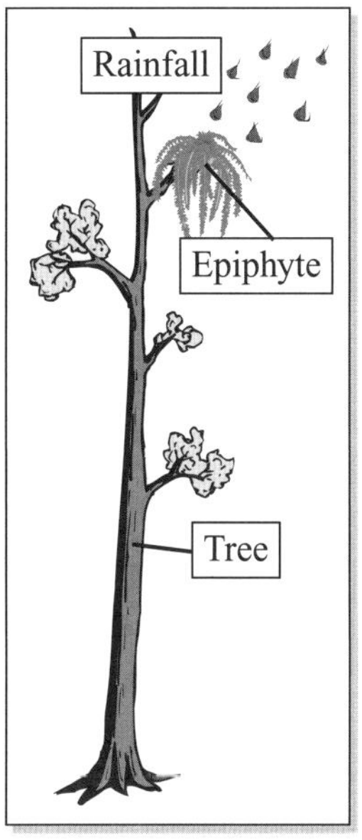

[3]

[Total 4 marks]

Topic 4 — Sustaining Ecosystems

Tropical Rainforests — Human Impacts

1 Study **Figure 1**, a graph showing the number of tourists visiting an area of tropical rainforest.

Figure 1

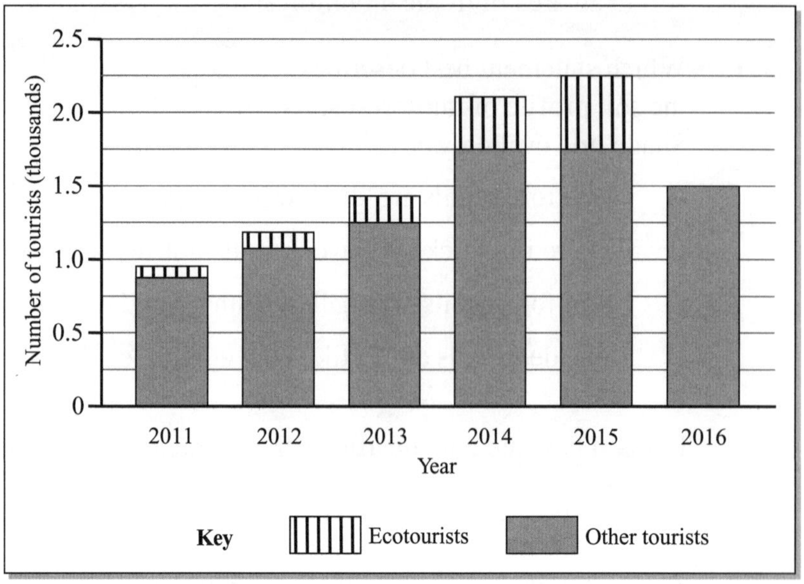

Always read the axis labels on graphs carefully so you are sure what's being measured and what the units are.

a) How many tourists in total visited the area in 2015?

....
[1]

b) Complete **Figure 1** to show that 750 ecotourists visited in 2016.
[1]

c) Explain how ecotourism can be part of a sustainable management strategy for a tropical rainforest.

....

....

....

....

....

....
[4]

d) Other than tourism opportunities, suggest why many people consider tropical rainforests to be a valuable resource.

....

....

....

....

....

....

....
[4]

[Total 10 marks]

Topic 4 — Sustaining Ecosystems

Tropical Rainforests — Human Impacts

2 Study **Figure 2**, a photograph showing gold mining in an area of tropical rainforest.

Figure 2

a) Using **Figure 2** and your own knowledge, explain the impacts of mineral extraction on tropical rainforests.

....

....

....

....

....

[3]

b) Outline **one** positive economic impact of logging.

....

....

[1]

c) Outline **two** environmental impacts of logging.

Impact 1:..

....

....

Impact 2:..

....

....

[4]

d) Explain how tropical rainforests can be managed to ensure timber can be extracted sustainably.

....

....

....

....

[2]

e) **Case study** — sustainable management of tropical rainforests

Name of tropical rainforest:..

Discuss the attempts to manage this rainforest sustainably.

[8 + 3 SPaG]

[Total 21 marks]

Polar Environments

1 Study **Figure 1**, a map of Antarctica.

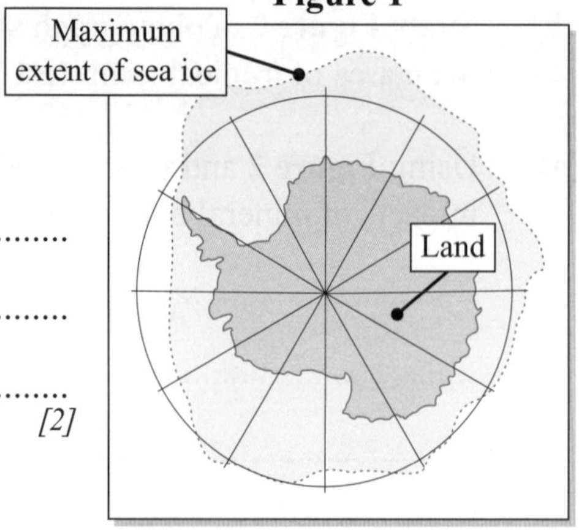

a) Using **Figure 1** and your own knowledge, describe the main features of the land and sea in the Antarctic.

....

....

....
[2]

Figure 1

Maximum extent of sea ice

Land

b) State **one** way in which the landscape of the Arctic differs from that of Antarctica.

....

....
[1]

c) Describe the differences in the flora of the Arctic and Antarctica.

....

....

....
[2]

[Total 5 marks]

2 Study **Figure 2**, a diagram showing interdependence in polar environments.

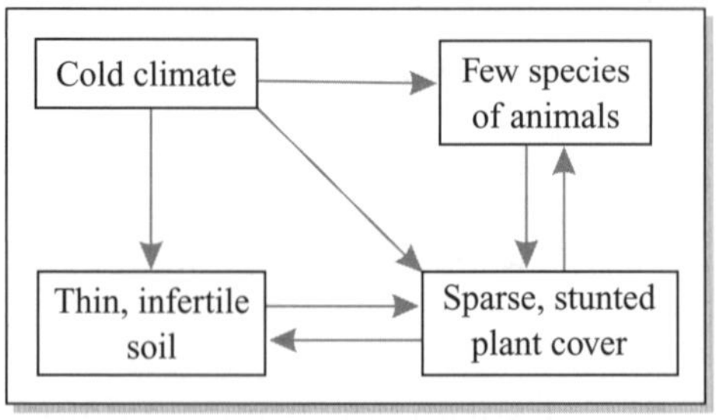

a) Using **Figure 2** and your own knowledge, explain why soils in polar environments are often thin and infertile.

....

....

....

....

....
[3]

Figure 2

Cold climate → Few species of animals

Thin, infertile soil → Sparse, stunted plant cover

b) Suggest how changes to ocean currents could threaten polar ecosystems.

....

....

....

....
[3]

[Total 6 marks]

Polar Environments — Human Impacts

1   Human activities have a variety of impacts on polar environments.

a)   Which **two** of the following statements best describe how fishing can have a negative impact on polar ecosystems? Shade **one** oval only.

1   Indigenous people often take more fish than they need, causing fish populations to decline.

2   Commercial overfishing is threatening some species with extinction.

3   Birds can get caught in fishing nets and drown.

4   Fishermen kill whales to stop them eating the fish they want to catch.

  A   1 and 2   ⬭

  B   2 and 3   ⬭

  C   1 and 4   ⬭

  D   3 and 4   ⬭

[1]

b)   Outline **one** possible impact that mineral exploitation may have on the environment in polar regions.

....

....

[2]

c)   Describe **two** impacts of tourism on the Arctic ecosystem.

....

....

....

....

....

[4]

d)   To what extent does scientific research in polar environments have a positive effect on ecosystems?

....

....

....

....

....

....

[6]

[Total 13 marks]

Polar Environments — Case Studies

1   Case study — small-scale example of sustainable management in either the Arctic or the Antarctic.

Example:..

Discuss the success of this example of sustainable management.

....

....

....

....

....

....

....

....

....

....

[Total 6 marks]

2   Case study — global sustainable management in the Arctic or the Antarctic.

Example:..

To what extent has this example of global management been successful?

....

....

....

....

....

....

....

....

....

....

[Total 6 marks]

Urban Growth

1   Study **Figure 1**, a graph showing the change in the urban population of richer countries (ACs) and poorer countries (EDCs and LIDCs) between 1960 and 2010.

a)   Complete the graph to show that the urban population of EDCs and LIDCs in 2010 was 2.72 billion.

[1]

Figure 1

b)   In 1960 the urban population of EDCs and LIDCs was 0.56 billion.
Calculate the percentage change in the urban population between 1960 and 2010.

....

....

....

....

[1]

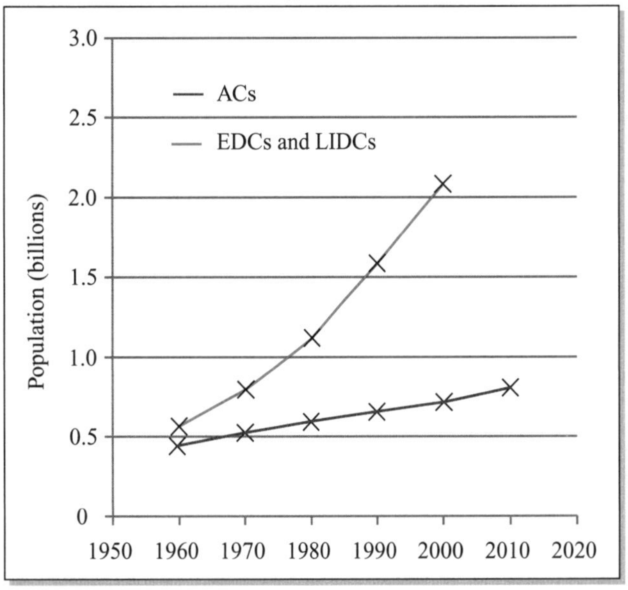

c)   Describe the trends shown in **Figure 1**.

....

....

....

....

....

[3]

d)   Suggest reasons for the difference in the rate of urbanisation in richer and poorer countries shown in **Figure 1**.

....

....

....

....

....

....

....

....

....

[6]

[Total 11 marks]

Urban Growth

2 Study **Figure 2**, which shows the global distribution of megacities in 1975 and 2014.

Figure 2

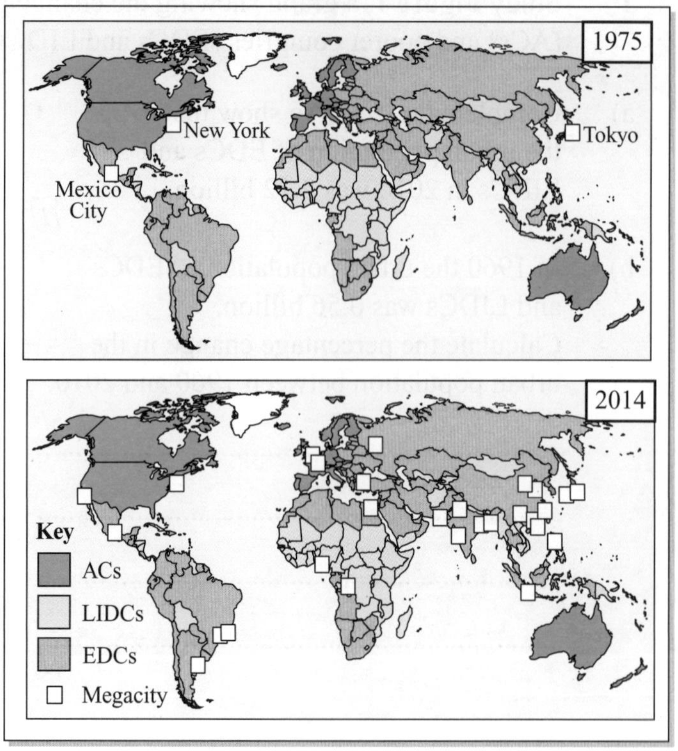

a) Which of the following statements is correct? Shade **one** oval only.

  A Megacities have a population of less than 10 000 people. ⬭

  B Megacities have a population of less than 1 million people. ⬭

  C Megacities have a population of more than 10 million people. ⬭

  D Megacities have a population of more than 100 million people. ⬭
  [1]

b) Describe the changes in the number and distribution of megacities between 1975 and 2014 shown in **Figure 2**.

  ....

  ....

  ....

  ....

  ....
  [3]

c) What is a world city?

  ....

  ....
  [1]

d) Which of the following is **not** a characteristic of world cities? Shade **one** oval only.

  A They have a low proportion of foreign-born people. ⬭

  B Lots of people and goods from international destinations pass through them. ⬭

  C They are centres for international media and culture. ⬭

  D They are centres for trade and business. ⬭
  [1]

e) Outline how the distribution of world cities has changed since 1950.

  ....

  ....

  ....
  [2]

  [Total 8 marks]

Urbanisation in LIDCs

1 Study the table showing the rural and urban populations of the Republic of the Congo in 1990 and 2014.

Figure 1

	Rural	Urban
1990	1100	1300
2014	1600	3000

Population in thousands

a) Calculate the ratio of the rural to urban population in the Republic of the Congo in 2014. Give your answer in its simplest form.

....

....

[1]

b) Suggest **two** pull factors that encourage people in LIDCs to move to cities from rural areas.

1:...

....

2:...

....

[2]

c) Explain how internal growth contributes to urbanisation.

....

....

....

....

....

[3]

d) Outline **one** social consequence of rapid urban growth in LIDCs.

....

....

....

[2]

e) Describe the environmental consequences of rapid urban growth in LIDCs.

....

....

....

....

....

....

[4]

[Total 12 marks]

Topic 5 — Urban Futures

Suburbanisation

1   There is a range of push and pull factors that lead
        to suburbanisation in advanced countries (ACs).

a)   What is suburbanisation?

    ....

    ....
                                                                                                              [1]

b)   Which **one** of the following is **not** a pull factor leading to suburbanisation? Shade **one** oval only.

    A   Planning laws outside the city centre are relaxed, so it's easier to build houses.   ◯

    B   Suburban areas have more green spaces, so quality of life is higher.   ◯

    C   Public transport is often good in suburban areas, so commuting is easy.   ◯

    D   Suburban areas have many nightclubs and bars, so entertainment is easily accessible.   ◯
                                                                                                              [1]

c)   Outline the push factors that contribute to suburbanisation in advanced countries (ACs).

    ....

    ....

    ....

    ....

    ....

    ....
                                                                                                              [4]

d)   Explain **one** way in which suburbanisation can have a negative impact on city centres.

    ....

    ....

    ....
                                                                                                              [2]

e)   Describe how suburbanisation can have negative consequences for the environment.

    ....

    ....

    ....

    ....

    ....

    ....
                                                                                                              [4]

                                                                                              [Total 12 marks]

Topic 5 — Urban Futures

Counter-Urbanisation

1 Study **Figure 1**, an extract from an article on Little Yeoton,
a rural village close to the city of Hamslow.

Figure 1

Little Yeoton was once a thriving agricultural village, its inhabitants working mostly in
farming or for local shops and amenities. Over the last 20 years, an influx of people from
the nearby city of Hamslow has changed all this. Little Yeoton now buzzes into life each
morning to the sound of commuters hurrying towards the train station or starting their cars
ready for the daily commute. The village, with its convenient road and rail transport links to
Hamslow, is an ideal location for those who want to work in the city but wish to avoid living
amongst pollution and crime. However, the impact that this counter-urbanisation is having
on Little Yeoton is a growing concern for those who've lived in the village for decades.

a) What is meant by the term 'counter-urbanisation'?

....
[1]

b) Identify **two** causes of counter-urbanisation described in **Figure 1**.

....

....

....

....
[2]

c) Outline **one** cause of counter-urbanisation not mentioned in **Figure 1**.

....

....
[1]

d) 'Counter-urbanisation is beneficial for rural areas.'
To what extent do you agree with this statement?

....

....

....

....

....

....

....

....

....
[6]

[Total 10 marks]

Topic 5 — Urban Futures

Re-Urbanisation

1 Study **Figure 1**, a table showing the population growth and business start-ups in four UK urban areas between 2004 and 2014.

a) Using **Figure 1**, which city is most likely to be experiencing re-urbanisation? Shade **one** oval only.

A   Bournemouth   ⬭

B   Wigan   ⬭

C   Swansea   ⬭

D   Sunderland   ⬭

[1]

Figure 1

	Population change (2004-2014)	Business start ups 2014 (per 10 000 of population)
Bournemouth	10.17%	51.30
Wigan	5.25%	37.23
Swansea	4.52%	32.48
Sunderland	-1.14%	30.16

b) Explain the causes of re-urbanisation in advanced countries (ACs).

....

....

....

....

....

....

[4]

c) Discuss how re-urbanisation in advanced countries (ACs) can affect urban areas.

....

....

....

....

....

....

....

....

....

....

[6]

[Total 11 marks]

Cities in Advanced Countries

1   Study **Figure 1**, a graph showing the migration of males into
     and out of London in 2013 across a range of age groups.

Figure 1

a)   Using **Figure 1**, which age group experienced
     a net increase in population due to migration?
     Shade **one** oval only.

     A   0-10 years   ⬭

     B   11-20 years   ⬭

     C   21-30 years   ⬭

     D   31-40 years   ⬭
                                              [1]

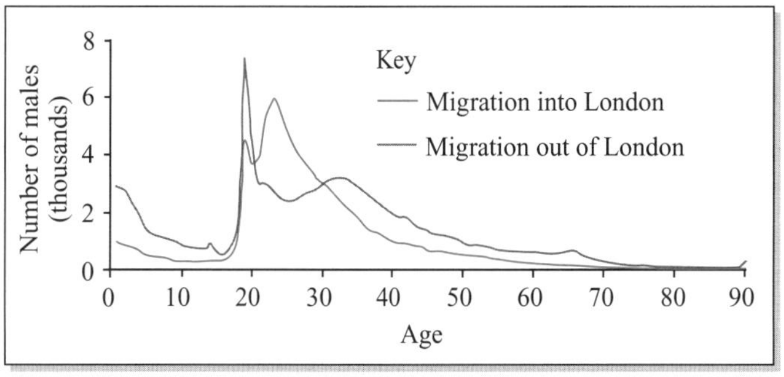

b)   What is meant by national migration?

     ....

     ....
                                                                                                        [1]

c)   Describe how international migration is changing the growth and character of a named AC city.

     ....

     ....

     ....

     ....

     ....
                                                                                                        [4]
                                                                                            [Total 6 marks]

2   Cities in advanced countries (ACs) face a range of challenges.

     Describe the challenges of transport provision in an AC city you have studied,
     and examine how these challenges affect life in the city.

     ....

     ....

     ....

     ....

     ....

     ....

     ....

     ....
                                                                                            [Total 6 marks]

Cities in Advanced Countries

3   Study **Figure 2**, a graph showing population change in London from 2004 to 2014 and **Figure 3**, a graph showing house prices and the number of new houses built in London from 2004 to 2016.

Figure 2

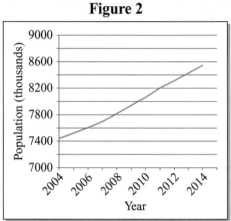

Figure 3

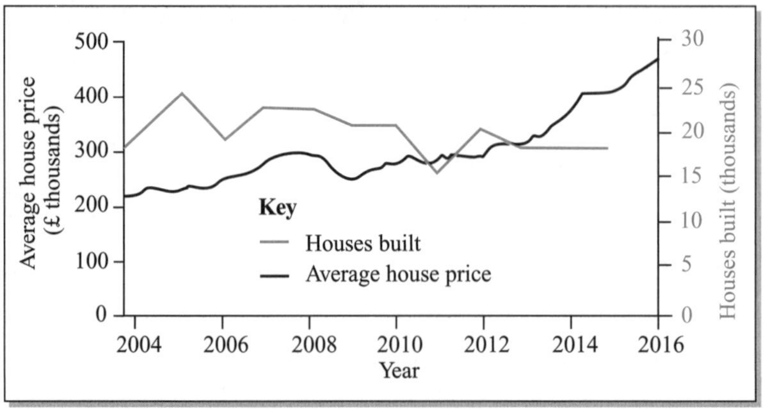

a)   Describe the trend in the population of London shown in **Figure 2**.

....
[1]

b)   Using **Figure 2** and **Figure 3**, suggest why London is facing a housing crisis.

....

....

....

....
[3]

c)   Describe the challenges created by inequality in an AC city you have studied, and outline how these challenges have affected life in the city.

....

....

....

....

....
[4]

d)   For a named AC city, describe **one** initiative that is being used to make it more sustainable.

....

....

....

....

....
[4]

[Total 12 marks]

Cities in Developing Countries

1 There are a number of challenges that affect life in LIDC and EDC cities.

a) Which of the following is **not** likely to be a challenge faced by a worker in the informal sector?
Shade **one** oval only.

    A   Working in dangerous conditions.   ◯

    B   Working long hours.   ◯

    C   Earning very little.   ◯

    D   Having to pay high taxes.   ◯   *[1]*

b) Describe the evidence shown in **Figure 1** for challenges faced by many LIDC and EDC cities.

Figure 1

....

....

....

....

....

....
[2]

c) Explain the health challenges that affect life in an EDC or LIDC city you have studied.

....

....

....

....

....

....
[4]

d) Describe how migration has affected the growth of a city in an EDC or an LIDC.

....

....

....

....
[3]

e) Examine how ways of life vary between **one** LIDC or EDC city and **one** AC city.

[8 + 3 SPaG]

[Total 21 marks]

Uneven Development

1   Study **Figure 1**, which shows measures of development for Canada, Malaysia and Angola.

a)   Which of the following is a measure of economic development?
Shade **one** oval only.

Figure 1

	Canada	Malaysia	Angola
GNI per capita	$51 770	$11 120	$4800
Birth rate	10.28	19.71	38.78
Death rate	8.42	5.03	11.49
Infant mortality rate	4.65	13.27	78.26
Life expectancy	81.76	74.75	55.63
Literacy rate	97.1%	94.6%	71.1%
HDI value	0.913	0.779	0.532

    A   GNI per capita   ⬭

    B   Birth rate   ⬭

    C   Life expectancy   ⬭

    D   Literacy rate   ⬭   *[1]*

b)   i)   Define birth rate.

....

[1]

    ii)   How might the differences in birth rates shown in **Figure 1** be a consequence of uneven development?

....

....

....

[2]

c)   What is meant by the Gross National Income (GNI) per capita of a country?

....

....

....

[2]

d)   Explain why the Human Development Index (HDI) values given in **Figure 1** may be a better measure of development than any of the other measures.

....

....

....

[2]

e)   Using **Figure 1**, suggest how uneven development might have consequences for the health of people in LIDCs.

....

....

....

....

....

[4]

Uneven Development

f)   Explain which of the countries shown in **Figure 1** is the most developed.

....

....

....

....

....

....

[4]

[Total 16 marks]

2   Study **Figure 2**, which shows the distribution of low-income developing countries (LIDCs), advanced countries (ACs) and emerging and developing countries (EDCs).

a)   Using **Figure 2**, describe the global distribution of LIDCs.

Figure 2

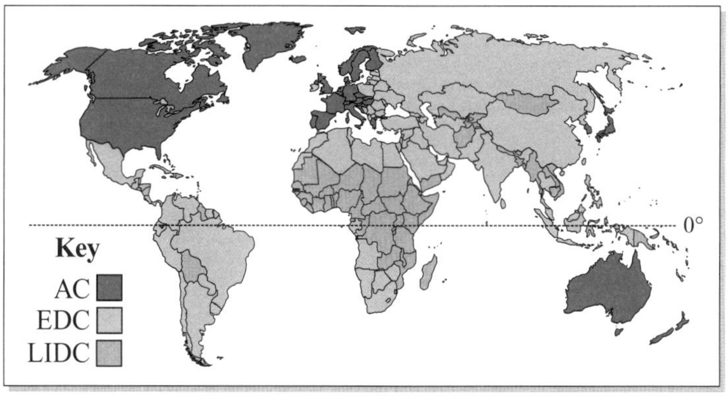

Key
AC
EDC
LIDC

....

....

....

....

....

....

....

[2]

b)   Which of the following is a characteristic of ACs? Shade **one** oval only.

A   Very rapidly expanding economy.   ◯

B   High life expectancy.   ◯

C   Low standard of living.   ◯

D   Limited exports of manufactured goods.   ◯

[1]

c)   Describe the characteristics of EDCs.

....

....

....

....

[3]

[Total 6 marks]

Factors Affecting Development

1   Study **Figure 1**, an article about Libya written in 2016.

Figure 1

Libya is the fourth largest country in Africa. It's located on the northern edge of the Sahara desert. More than 90% of the country is a desert or semi-desert environment.

There has been ongoing conflict in Libya since 2011, leading to economic decline and worsening living standards. GDP per capita has decreased by about 30% since 2013.

Oil is an important industry in Libya. It accounts for 97% of the country's exports and 80% of Libya's GDP. However, oil companies started to leave the country after the outbreak of violence.

a)   Using **Figure 1**, explain how climate may have affected the level of development of Libya.

....

....

....

....

....

....
                                                                                                                    [4]

b)   Outline **two** other physical factors that can affect how developed a country is.

1:..

....

2:..

....
                                                                                                                    [4]

c)   Using **Figure 1**, suggest how conflict may have affected Libya's level of development.

....

....

....

....

....

....
                                                                                                                    [4]
                                                                                                          [Total 12 marks]

Factors Affecting Development

2 In 2014, Nicaragua had a 0.03% share of the world's total exports while the UK had a 2.66% share. Study **Figure 2**, which shows the types of goods exported by each country.

Figure 2

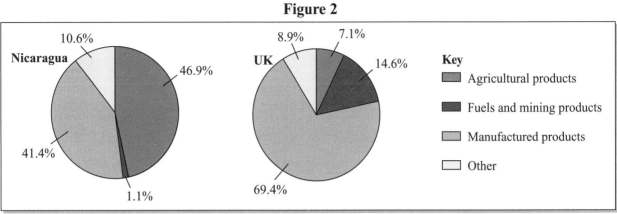

a) In 2014, what percentage of UK exports was not agricultural products, fuels or mining products?

....

[1]

b) In 2014, Nicaragua generated US $5.1 million from exports. Using **Figure 2**, calculate how much money was generated from the export of manufactured products.

....

[1]

c) Explain how poor trade links might make it difficult for a country to break out of poverty.

....

....

....

[2]

d) Using **Figure 2**, suggest a reason why Nicaragua is less developed than the UK.

....

....

....

[2]

e) Outline how debt can make it difficult for a country to break out of poverty.

....

....

....

[2]

[Total 8 marks]

Factors Affecting Development

3 Answer the following questions using a case study of economic development in a low-income developing country (LIDC).

a) For an LIDC you have studied, explain how political and social factors have affected the level of development.

....

....

....

....

....

....

....

....

....

....

[6]

b) For an LIDC you have studied, examine how the environment may have affected the level of development.

....

....

....

....

....

....

....

....

....

....

[6]

[Total 12 marks]

Increasing Development — Stages and Goals

1   Study **Figure 1**, which shows Rostow's model of the stages of economic development.

a)   Which of the following features is a
defining characteristic of Stage 3 of
Rostow's model (Take-off)?
Shade **one** oval only.

Figure 1

    A   Widespread use
of technology.   ⬭

    B   Subsistence farming.   ⬭

    C   Manufacturing starts to
develop.   ⬭

    D   Large-scale
industrialisation.   ⬭

[1]

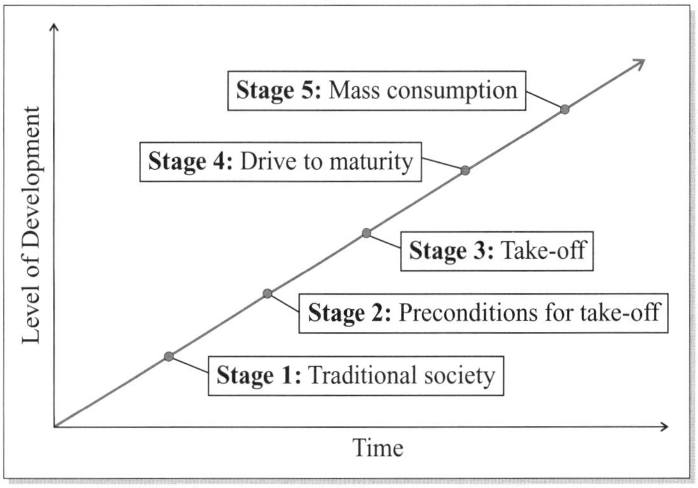

b)   Which statement best describes Stage 4 of Rostow's model (Drive to maturity)?
Shade **one** oval only.

    A   Manufacturing industries begin to develop, along with the infrastructure
needed to support them.   ⬭

    B   The population becomes increasingly wealthy, the use of technology
increases and standards of living rise.   ⬭

    C   The economy is largely subsistence-based and there is very little
international trade.   ⬭

    D   Goods are mass produced, and the wealthy population
means that levels of consumption are very high.   ⬭

[1]

c)   For an LIDC you have studied, discuss how closely its path of
economic development fits Rostow's model.

....

....

....

....

....

....

[4]

d)   To what extent have the Millennium Development Goals been met in an LIDC that
you have studied?

[8 + 3 SPaG]

[Total 17 marks]

Topic 6 — Dynamic Development

Increasing Development — Trade and TNCs

1   Study **Figure 1**, which shows the global distribution of sites of a Trans-National Company (TNC).

Figure 1

Key
■ AC   ■ EDC   ■ LIDC
★ Headquarters   ◆ Research and development sites   ○ Offices   ■ Factories

a)   Using **Figure 1**, where are most factories located?
Shade **one** oval only.

  A   ACs   ○
  B   EDCs   ○
  C   LIDCs   ○
  D   ACs and LIDCs   ○
  [1]

b)   Which statement best describes a benefit of TNC investment for LIDCs?
Shade **one** oval only.

  A   TNCs bring in workers from other countries to do skilled jobs.   ○
  B   New technology is developed in ACs.   ○
  C   TNCs send money back to their country of origin.   ○
  D   Employees get a more reliable income.   ○
  [1]

c)   Which statement best describes a benefit of international trade for LIDCs?
Shade **one** oval only.

  A   It provides jobs for local people.   ○
  B   It pushes wages and working conditions down.   ○
  C   It encourages the country to rely on exporting primary products.   ○
  D   It increases the country's dependence on trading one product.   ○
  [1]

d)   Outline the problems that taking part in international trade might cause for LIDCs.

....

....

....

....

....

....

  [4]

e)   For an LIDC you have studied, to what extent have Trans-National Companies (TNCs) improved economic development and quality of life?

  [8 + 3 SPaG]

  [Total 18 marks]

Increasing Development — Strategies

1   Study **Figure 1**, an article about an aid project in Ghana.

Figure 1

> ## UK Government Support for Ghana
>
> The UK is the second largest aid donor to Ghana. The UK Government's Department for International Development (DFID) gave over £205 million between 2005 and 2007 towards Ghana's poverty reduction plans. This level of aid continues, with donations of around £85 million per year. The aid is used in several ways, including to improve healthcare, education and sanitation.
>
> About 15% of the UK's funding in 2008 was used to support the healthcare system in Ghana —
>
> £42.5 million was pledged to support the Ghanaian Government's 2008-2012 health plan. On top of that, in 2008 the UK gave nearly £7 million to buy emergency equipment to reduce maternal deaths.
>
> Thanks to a £105 million grant from the UK in 2006, Ghana has been able to set up a ten year education strategic plan. It was the first African country to do this. The UK pledged additional money to help 12 000 children in North Ghana to get a formal basic education.

a)   Which of the statements below best describes the aid projects described in **Figure 1**? Shade **one** oval only.

    A   Short-term, 'top-down' aid   ◯

    B   Short-term, 'bottom-up' aid   ◯

    C   Long-term, 'top-down' aid   ◯

    D   Long-term, 'bottom-up' aid   ◯   *[1]*

b)   Outline **one** potential advantage and **one** potential disadvantage for the recipient country of long-term aid projects.

    Advantage:..

    ....

    Disadvantage:..

    ....

    [2]

c)   Outline **one** potential advantage and **one** potential disadvantage for the recipient country of short-term aid projects.

    Advantage:..

    ....

    Disadvantage:..

    ....

    [2]

d)   For an LIDC you have studied, evaluate the success of **one** top-down and **one** bottom-up development strategy.

                                                              [8 + 3 SPaG]

                                                                 [Total 16 marks]

Topic 7 — UK in the 21st Century

Characteristics of the UK

1 Study **Figure 1** and **Figure 2**, which show rainfall and population density in the UK.

Figure 1

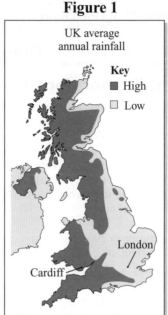

Figure 2

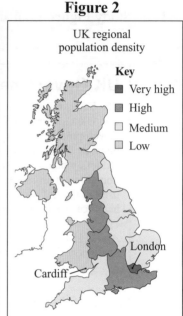

a) Which of these statements is correct? Shade **one** oval only.

   A   The south of the UK receives little rain. ◯

   B   Rainfall is higher in Cardiff than in London. ◯

   C   Rainfall is higher in the east of the UK than in the west. ◯

   D   Scotland generally has low rainfall. ◯

   [1]

b) Describe the pattern of population density in the UK.

   ....

   ....

   ....
   [2]

c) Explain how patterns of rainfall and population density may cause problems in south-east England.

   ....

   ....

   ....

   ....
   [3]

d) Study **Figure 3**, which shows land use in the UK. Which **two** statements about land use are correct? Shade **one** oval only.

   1   Most of the UK is urban.

   2   Agricultural land covers more of the UK land than wetlands.

   3   A high proportion of Scotland is natural land.

   4   Urban areas are concentrated in Wales.

Figure 3

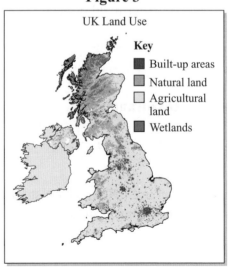

   A   1 and 3   ◯

   B   2 and 3   ◯

   C   2 and 4   ◯

   D   3 and 4   ◯

   [1]
   [Total 7 marks]

The Changing Population of the UK

1   Study **Figure 1**, population pyramids for the UK for 2001 and 2015.

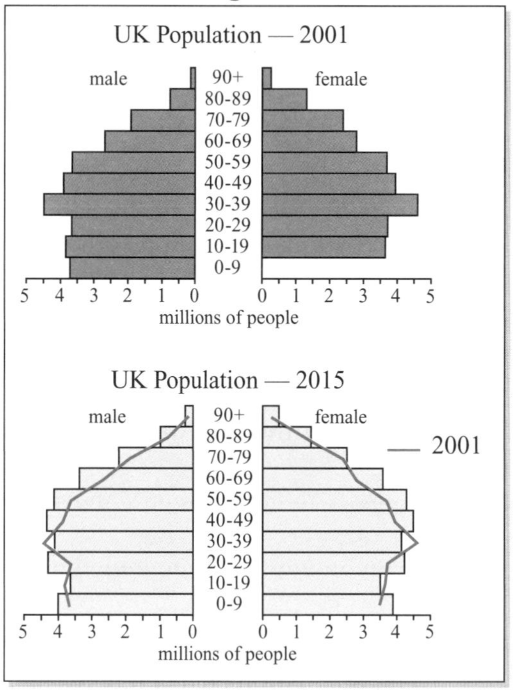

a)   Complete **Figure 1** to show that there were 3 500 000 girls aged 0-9 years old in 2001.

[1]

b)   How many people aged 40-49 were there in the UK in 2001?

....

[1]

c)   What is the modal class of the UK population in 2001?

....

[1]

d)   Using **Figure 1**, describe how the age structure of the UK population changed from 2001 to 2015.

....

....

....

....

[3]

[Total 6 marks]

Figure 1

UK Population — 2001

UK Population — 2015

2   Study **Figure 2**, which shows the demographic transition model, together with UK birth and death rates for 2015.

Figure 2

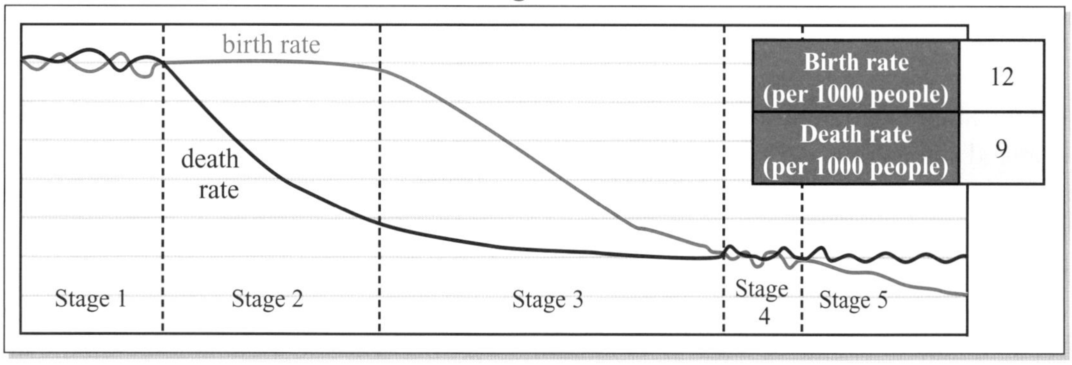

| Birth rate (per 1000 people) | 12 |
| Death rate (per 1000 people) | 9 |

Suggest what stage of the demographic transition model the UK is at.
Use **Figure 2** to justify your answer.

....

....

....

....

[Total 3 marks]

Topic 7 — UK in the 21st Century

The Changing Population of the UK

3 Study **Figure 3**, a table showing population change in the UK from 2001 and 2015.

a) What was the net number of migrants to the UK in 2012?

....
[1]

b) Calculate the range of the net international migration values.

....
[1]

c) Calculate the percentage change in internal growth between 2011 and 2015.

....

....
[1]

d) Using only **Figure 3**, describe how the UK population changed between 2001 and 2015 and what caused this change.

Figure 3

	Internal growth (births – deaths)	Net international migration	Overall net change
2001	74 300	153 200	227 500
2002	61 700	190 900	252 600
2003	76 700	194 200	270 900
2004	103 800	209 900	313 700
2005	127 000	336 000	463 000
2006	159 000	254 800	413 800
2007	187 100	304 900	492 000
2008	220 600	284 100	504 700
2009	216 700	220 100	436 800
2010	243 300	255 600	498 900
2011	255 200	270 500	525 700
2012	254 400	165 500	419 900
2013	212 100	188 500	400 600
2014	226 200	264 900	491 100
2015	171 800	341 400	513 200

....

....

....

....

....

....
[4]

e) For a named location in the UK, describe how its population structure and ethnic diversity have changed since 2001.

....

....

....

....

....

....

....

....
[6]

[Total 13 marks]

The UK's Ageing Population

1   Study **Figure 1**, a map of the UK showing the proportion of people over the age of 65.

a)   Describe the distribution of older people in the UK.

Figure 1

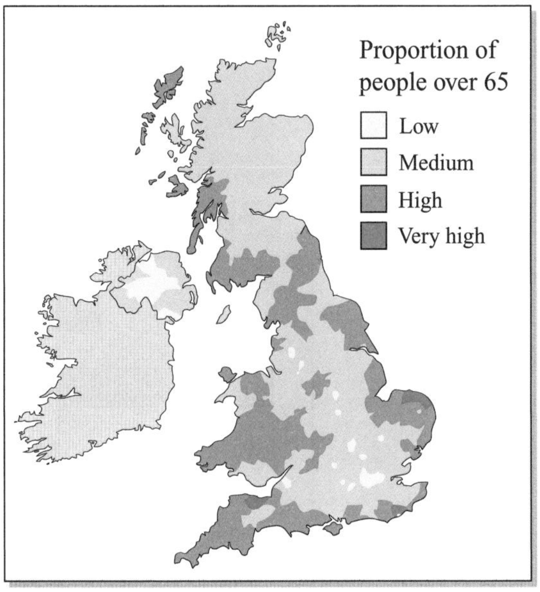

Proportion of
people over 65

☐ Low
☐ Medium
■ High
■ Very high

....

....

....

....

....

....

....

....

....
[3]

b)   Which of the following is **NOT** a cause of the UK's ageing population? Shade **one** oval only.

A   Low birth rates.   ⬯

B   Better healthcare.   ⬯

C   Increased age of retirement.   ⬯

D   Healthier lifestyles.   ⬯
[1]

c)   Describe the effect an ageing population has on the UK.

....

....

....

....

....

....
[4]

d)   Outline the possible responses to the UK's ageing population.

....

....

....

....
[3]

[Total 11 marks]

The Changing Economy of the UK

1   Study **Figure 1**, a graph showing change in the percentage of people employed in different sectors in the UK between 2001 and 2014.

Figure 1

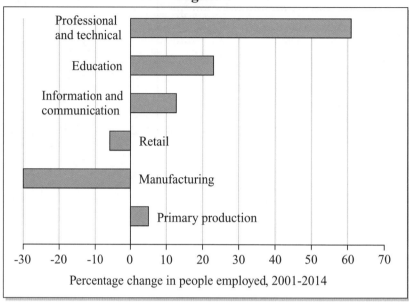

Percentage change in people employed, 2001-2014

a)   Use **Figure 1** to complete the following sentences.

i)   The sector with the greatest percentage decrease in employment was ....
[1]

ii)   The percentage of people employed in education increased by ....
[1]

iii)   The biggest percentage increase was in the .... sector.
[1]

b)   Describe how employment in different sectors changed between 2001 and 2014.

....

....

....

....
[3]

c)   Suggest how changing political priorities might have affected the UK economy since 2001.

....

....

....

....

....

....
[4]

[Total 10 marks]

UK Economic Hubs

1 Study **Figure 1**, which shows part of London's financial district. London is an economic hub.

a) Describe what an economic hub is.

Figure 1

....

....

....

....

....
[2]

b) Which of the following statements about the distribution of economic hubs in the UK is true?
Shade **one** oval only.

    A   Economic hubs are usually in rural areas. ⬭

    B   Most economic hubs are in northern Scotland. ⬭

    C   There are no economic hubs in Wales. ⬭

    D   There are lots of economic hubs in
        south-east England. ⬭
[1]

c) Which of the following is **not** a reason why a company might choose to locate in central London?
Shade **one** oval only.

    A   Transport links are good. ⬭

    B   Land is cheap. ⬭

    C   There are plenty of skilled workers. ⬭

    D   There are lots of other businesses there. ⬭
[1]

d) For an economic hub that you have studied, discuss how its economy has changed over time.

....

....

....

....

....

....

....

....

....
[6]

[Total 10 marks]

Topic 7 — UK in the 21st Century

The UK's Role in the World

1 Use your knowledge of the UK's role in international organisations to answer the following questions.

a) Name **one** international organisation of which the UK is a member.

....

[1]

b) Explain the purpose of the organisation you named in part a).

....

....

....

[2]

c) Which of the following is **NOT** normally a purpose of international organisations?
Shade **one** oval only.

A   To help less developed countries to develop.   ⬭

B   To find peaceful resolutions to conflicts.   ⬭

C   To increase the security of member states.   ⬭

D   To punish countries that are not members.   ⬭

[1]

d) For a global conflict you have studied, explain how the UK played a role in the conflict through its involvement with international organisations.

....

....

....

....

....

....

....

....

....

....

[6]

[Total 10 marks]

UK Media Exports

1   Study **Figure 1**, which shows the top ten countries by box office takings for the 2012 UK film 'Skyfall'.

Figure 1

	Box office takings (million US $)
USA	304.4
UK	158.3
Germany	85.2
France	59.1
China	59.0
Australia	50.8
Japan	30.6
Netherlands	23.0
Russia	22.8
Switzerland	20.2

a)   Calculate how much more money was taken in the USA than in the UK.

   ....
   [1]

b)   In total, 'Skyfall' made US $1110 million at the box office. Calculate the percentage of total box office takings that came from the UK.

   ....

   ....
   [1]

c)   **Figure 2** shows tourists in the UK photographing a set from a 'Harry Potter' film. Using **Figure 2**, explain how media exports might encourage people to visit the UK.

Figure 2

   ....

   ....

   ....

   ....

   ....
   [2]

d)   Using **Figure 1**, **Figure 2** and your own knowledge, explain how UK films have a global influence.

   ....

   ....

   ....

   ....

   ....

   ....

   ....

   ....

   ....
   [6]

   [Total 10 marks]

Multicultural UK

1 Study **Figure 1**, which shows a road in Harrow, north London.

Using **Figure 1**, describe how ethnic groups have contributed to UK culture by influencing food.

Figure 1

....

....

....

....

....

....

[Total 3 marks]

Figure 2

2 Study **Figure 2**, which shows a samba band playing in a parade in Omagh, Northern Ireland.

Using **Figure 2**, describe how ethnic groups have contributed to UK culture by influencing media.

....

....

....

....

....

....

[Total 3 marks]

3 Study **Figure 3**, which shows a shop selling Asian clothing in Coventry.

Using **Figure 3**, describe how ethnic groups have contributed to UK culture by influencing fashion.

Figure 3

....

....

....

....

....

[Total 3 marks]

Resource Supply and Demand

1   Study **Figure 1**, a graph showing real and projected changes in global population from 1950 to 2050.

Figure 1

a)   Using **Figure 1** and your own knowledge, describe how changes in global population are affecting demand for resources.

....

....

....

....

....

....

....

....

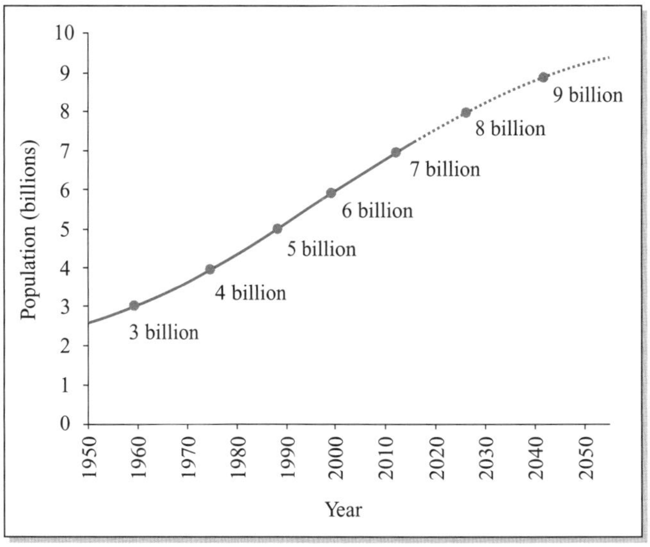

[3]

b)   Outline **one** other factor that is affecting global demand for resources.

....

....

....

....

[2]

c)   Suggest **one** factor that may limit water supply. Give a reason for your answer.

....

....

....

....

[2]

d)   Suggest **one** factor that may limit energy supply. Give a reason for your answer.

....

....

....

....

[2]

[Total 9 marks]

Human Use of the Environment

1 Study **Figure 1**, a photo of a farmer spraying chemicals on crops.

Figure 1

a) Using **Figure 1**, describe **one** way that farming practices have changed since the 1960s and explain how this has helped to increase food supply.

....

....

....

....

....

....

[2]

b) Describe the environmental impact of changing farming practices.

....

....

....

....

[3]

[Total 5 marks]

2 Study **Figure 2**, a table showing forest cover in Terra Spoglio between 1970 and 2010.

a) Using **Figure 2**, calculate the percentage change in forest cover between 1970 and 2010.

....

....

....

[1]

Figure 2

Year	Area of forest cover remaining (million ha)
1970	5.42
1980	5.40
1990	4.89
2000	4.61
2010	4.04

b) The total area of Terra Spoglio is 19 million hectares. What percentage of Terra Spoglio was covered by forest in 1990?

....

[1]

c) Describe how deforestation can increase energy supply.

....

....

....

[2]

Human Use of the Environment

d) Outline the environmental impacts of mining fossil fuels to increase energy supply.

....

....

....

....

....

....

[4]

[Total 8 marks]

3 Study **Figure 3**, which shows population density in Huffland and average monthly rainfall at **two** settlements in the region.

Figure 3

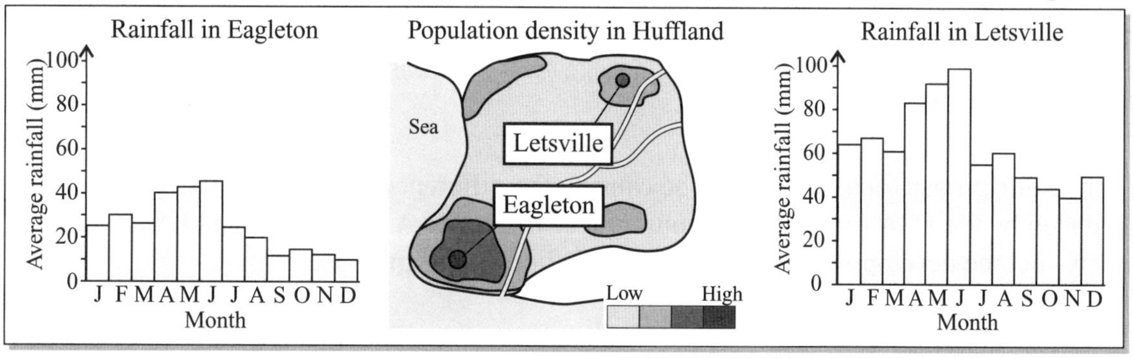

a) Using **Figure 3**, explain why a water transfer scheme might be necessary in Huffland.

....

....

....

[2]

b) Which of the following is a likely environmental impact of water transfer? Shade **one** oval only.

A   Some people may be left without enough water.   ◯

B   Engineering works, such as building pipes and canals, can damage ecosystems.   ◯

C   Flood risk increases in the area which water is transferred to.   ◯

D   Water level in rivers decreases, so there is more erosion of river banks.   ◯   *[1]*

c) Other than water transfer, describe **one** large-scale way of increasing water supply and explain how it could help make water supply in Eagleton more reliable.

....

....

....

....

[3]

[Total 6 marks]

Topic 8 — Resource Reliance

74

Food Security

1   Study **Figure 1**, which shows the production of cereals by country from 2012 to 2014.

a)   Using **Figure 1**, describe the
distribution of countries that
produced less than 2.8 million
tonnes of cereals from 2012 to 2014.

....

....

....

....

....

....

....

[2]

Figure 1

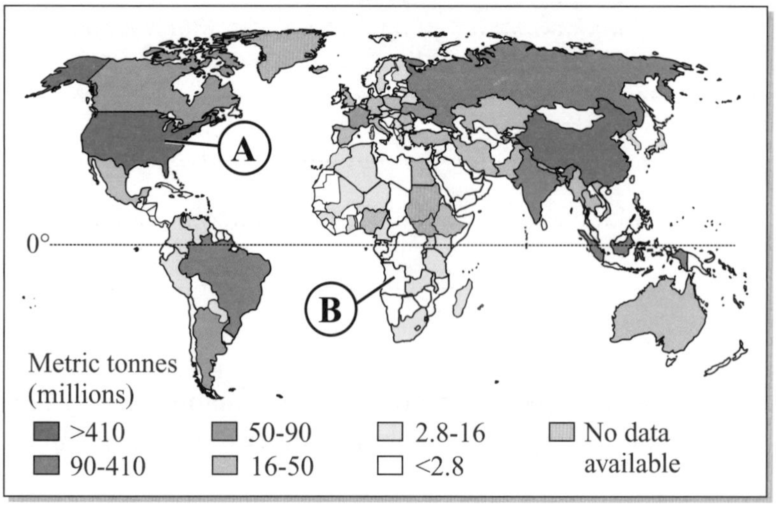

Metric tonnes (millions)
- >410
- 90-410
- 50-90
- 16-50
- 2.8-16
- <2.8
- No data available

b)   Outline **one** human factor that could be causing the difference in the quantity of cereals
produced by the USA (an advanced country (AC), labelled A in **Figure 1**) and Angola
(a low-income developing country (LIDC), labelled B in **Figure 1**).

....

....

....

[2]

c)   Describe what food security means.

....

....

[1]

d)   Explain the physical factors that can contribute to food insecurity.

....

....

....

....

....

....

[4]

[Total 9 marks]

Topic 8 — Resource Reliance

Access to Food

1 Study **Figure 1**, which shows average daily calorie intake per person around the world.

Figure 1

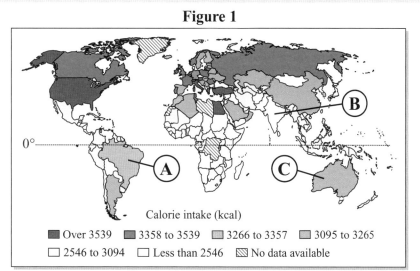

a) Which of the following statements about calorie intake is correct? Shade **one** oval only.

   A   Daily calorie intake is lower in Country A than in Country C.   ⬭

   B   Daily calorie intake in Country B is 3095 to 3265 kcal.   ⬭

   C   Daily calorie intake in Country A is 3266 to 3357 kcal.   ⬭

   D   Daily calorie intake is highest in Country C.   ⬭   *[1]*

b) Which of the following statements best describes what the Global Hunger Index shows? Shade **one** oval only.

   A   The amount of food that people eat in different countries.   ⬭

   B   How many people have access to food in different countries.   ⬭

   C   How much food people can afford to buy in different countries.   ⬭

   D   How many people are affected by lack of food in different countries.   ⬭   *[1]*

c) Compare Malthus's and Boserup's theories about how population growth and food availability are linked.

....

....

....

....

....

....

....

....

[6]

[Total 8 marks]

Topic 8 — Resource Reliance

Increasing Food Production

1 Study **Figure 1**, a graph showing the area of land used to grow organic crops in Finland from 1999 to 2015.

a) Describe how the area of land used to grow organic crops changed from 1999 to 2015.

Figure 1

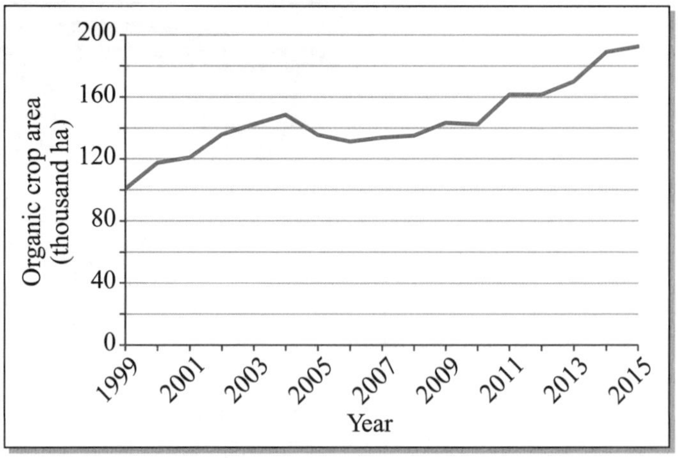

Organic crop area (thousand ha) vs Year

....

....

....

....

....

....

[2]

b) Outline **one** way in which organic farming is environmentally sustainable.

....

....

....

[2]

c) Which of the following is a way of intensifying farming? Shade **one** oval only.

A   Reducing the amount of resources used.   ⬭

B   Increasing the size of the area in which food is produced.   ⬭

C   Increasing the amount of chemicals used on crops.   ⬭

D   Ensuring animals have access to outside space.   ⬭   *[1]*

d) Assess how far technological developments that increase food production are sustainable.

....

....

....

....

....

....

....

....

....

[6]

[Total 11 marks]

Ethical Consumerism

1   Study **Figure 1**, which shows the annual income of a farmer in Mali between 2006 and 2014. He joined a fair trade cooperative in 2008.

a)   In 2014, the farmer earned £490.
     Complete the graph using this information.

     [1]

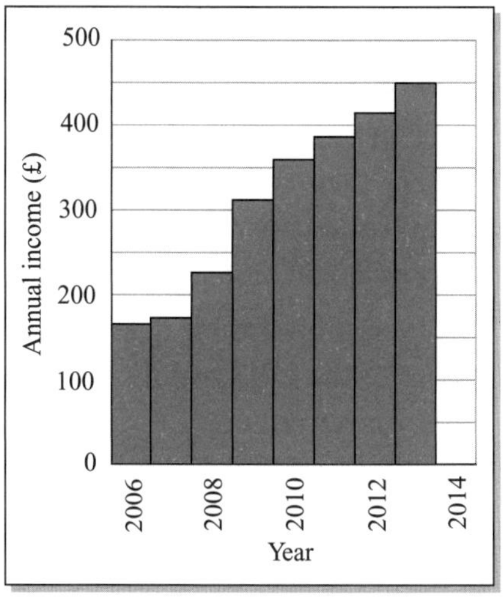

b)   What was the farmer's income in 2011?

     ....
     [1]

c)   Calculate the increase in the farmer's annual income from 2008 to 2014.

     ....

     ....
     [1]

Figure 1

[A bar chart titled "Figure 1" with y-axis "Annual income (£)" ranging from 0 to 500 and x-axis "Year" from 2006 to 2014.]

d)   Explain why an ethical consumer might prefer to buy fairly traded goods.

     ....

     ....

     ....

     ....

     ....
     [3]

e)   Other than buying fairly traded goods, outline **one** way of making food consumption more ethical.

     ....

     ....

     ....
     [2]

f)   Explain how ethical consumerism can help to increase food security.

     ....

     ....

     ....

     ....

     ....

     ....
     [4]

     [Total 12 marks]

Small-Scale Food Production

1 Study **Figure 1**, which gives information about an urban garden project.

Figure 1

Incredible Edible is an urban garden project that was started in 2007 in the town of Todmorden, West Yorkshire. The idea behind the project is to transform public spaces into urban garden plots, where people can get involved in growing their own produce.

The project founders wanted to encourage people to think about where their food comes from and whether it's sustainable. By creating tiny garden spaces all over the town, the residents of Todmorden have increased access to locally grown fruits and vegetables.

Incredible Edible Todmorden has led to the creation of similar projects all over the UK, and it's also been adopted by organisations in Europe and further afield.

a) Explain how urban gardens have increased food security in Todmorden.

....

....

....

[2]

b) Which **two** statements best describe some of the benefits of urban gardens? Shade **one** oval only.

1 They encourage people to eat more animal products, improving people's health.

2 They add greenery to cities, making them more attractive places to live.

3 They increase the amount of food than can be sourced locally, reducing transport distances.

4 They are run by the government, so they are available to everyone.

    A   1 and 2   ◯

    B   1 and 3   ◯

    C   2 and 3   ◯

    D   2 and 4   ◯   *[1]*

c) Other than urban gardens, describe **one** small-scale, bottom-up approach to increasing food production and explain how it is sustainable.

....

....

....

....

....

....

[4]

[Total 7 marks]

Topic 8 — Resource Reliance

Food Security — Case Study

1 Study **Figure 1**, a graph of average daily calorie intake in the UK from 1940 to 2000.

Figure 1

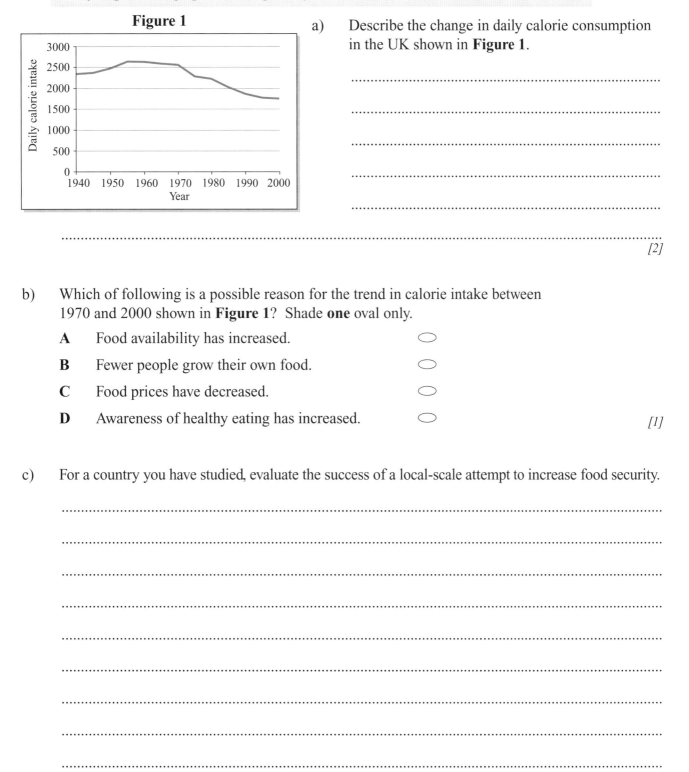

a) Describe the change in daily calorie consumption in the UK shown in **Figure 1**.

....

....

....

....

....

....

[2]

b) Which of following is a possible reason for the trend in calorie intake between 1970 and 2000 shown in **Figure 1**? Shade **one** oval only.

A	Food availability has increased.	⬭
B	Fewer people grow their own food.	⬭
C	Food prices have decreased.	⬭
D	Awareness of healthy eating has increased.	⬭

[1]

c) For a country you have studied, evaluate the success of a local-scale attempt to increase food security.

....

....

....

....

....

....

....

....

....

....

....

[6]

d) For a country you have studied, compare the effectiveness of one past and one present attempt to increase food security at a national scale.

[8 + 3 SPaG]

[Total 20 marks]

Decision-Making Exercise

Figure 1: Climate graph for Malawi

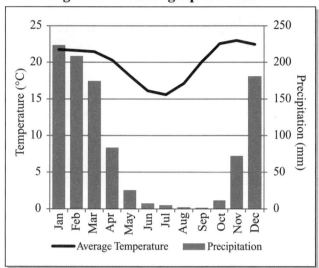

Figure 2: World map

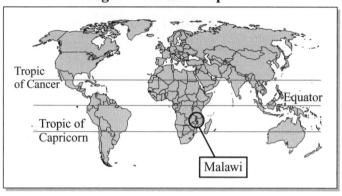

Figure 3: Effects of climate change

Human activities are thought to be contributing to climate change. Models suggest that climate change could raise global temperatures by 1-2 °C by 2100, if not more.

This is expected to cause precipitation patterns to change, with some areas seeing an increase in droughts and others seeing more frequent and extreme flooding.

Figure 4: Areas predicted to have a reduced water supply by 2040

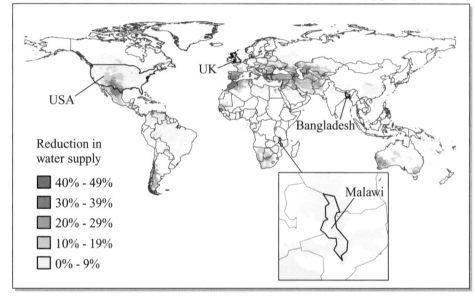

Figure 5: Predicted changes in crop yields by 2050

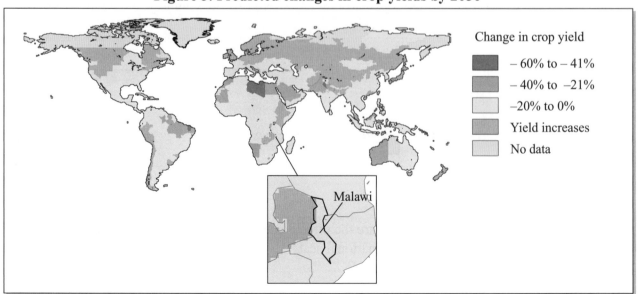

Decision-Making Exercise

Figure 6: Population and development indicators for four countries

	Population (millions)	GNI per capita (US $)	HDI*	Global Hunger Index◆	Access to safe water
UK	65	43 350	0.907	n/a	100%
USA	319	54 400	0.915	n/a	99%
Bangladesh	159	1080	0.570	27.3	87%
Malawi	17	360	0.445	27.3	90%

* Human Development Index (HDI) is a number between 0 and 1.
The closer to 1 the number is, the more developed a country is considered to be.

◆ Global Hunger Index is a number between 0 and 100 that measures hunger in EDCs and LIDCs. The scale ranks the severity of the problem from 'low' to 'extremely alarming' — scores from 20 to 34.9 indicate a 'serious' hunger problem.

Figure 7: Graph showing the percentage of children under 5 in Malawi suffering from undernutrition

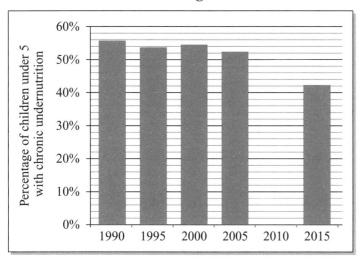

Figure 9: Comments on farming in Malawi

This summer, the rains were really heavy and my land flooded again. All my crops were destroyed. *Subsistence farmer, southern Malawi*

The droughts meant that crop yields were much lower this year. Now food is so expensive, I can't afford to buy enough to keep my family healthy. *City dweller, Lilongwe*

It's hard to grow food at the camp. The World Food Programme hands out the basics we need to keep going but there are about 23,000 people to feed. *Refugee from war in Burundi, Dzaleka refugee camp, central Malawi*

We eat any fish I can't sell. It gives my children the nutrients they need to grow properly. *Fisherman, Lake Malawi*

Figure 8: Facts about farming in Malawi

Most of the population live in rural areas. Agriculture is the biggest employment sector, but almost all the rural population are also involved in subsistence farming (growing food for personal use).

Rural population	80%
Employment in agriculture	60%
Contribution of agriculture to GDP	33%
People involved in subsistence farming	90% of rural population
Natural vegetation	Savannah grasslands, deciduous forest
Main export crops	Tobacco, tea, sugarcane
Main subsistence crop	Maize
Farming methods	Slash and burn* used to clear land. Move on after 2-3 years, when land becomes unproductive.

* *Slash and burn is a technique where vegetation is cut down and burnt so that crops can be planted.*

Figure 7 and Global Hunger Index values in Figure 6 source: von Grebmer et al. (2015). Reproduced with permission from the International Food Policy Research Institute.

Decision-Making Exercise

Figure 10: Changes in land use in Malawi 1990-2013

	1990	2013
Forest cover	41.3%	33.8%
Agricultural land	44.7%	61.4%

Figure 11: Photographs of life in Malawi

A traditional cooking fire

Drying tobacco leaves, one of Malawi's largest sources of income

A typical Malawian village

Figure 12: Examples of current food security projects in Malawi

Food banks
The Hunger Project operates eight food banks distributed throughout Malawi. These have food stocks to ensure local communities have enough food all year round, even if they are affected by droughts or floods. Three of the food banks provide equipment so that farmers can process their crops and sell them for more money. Most also distribute fertiliser, so that farmers can increase their crop yields. However, the food banks currently reach less than 1% of the population.

Subsidies
In 2004, the government began offering subsidies to enable poor farmers to buy fertilisers and seed. This triggered a 'green revolution', massively increasing Malawi's maize production. However, the system collapsed because foreign donors pulled out and the government could no longer afford the subsidies. The government has continued to promote maize production over the diversification of crops.

Permaculture
Organisations such as the African Moringa and Permaculture Project are working with local communities to help them develop more reliable food supplies. For example, they are training local communities in permaculture principles. They also help local community groups develop products such as peanut butter to sell at a higher price. However, the project is in its early stages and needs funding to develop further.

Decision-Making Exercise

1   Study **Figures 1** and **2** on page 80, a graph of Malawi's climate and a map of the world.

a)   Use **Figure 1** to complete the sentences below.

i)   The month with the lowest average temperature is ....

[1]

ii)   The month with the most precipitation is ....

[1]

b)   Using **Figures 1** and **2**, describe the climate of Malawi and explain how this may be influenced by Malawi's location.

....

....

....

....

....

....

....

....

....

[6]

[Total 8 marks]

2   Study **Figures 3**, **4**, **5** and **6** on pages 80-81, information about climate change, maps of predicted change in water supply and crop yield, and a table of development indicators.

a)   Using **Figure 4**, describe the pattern of predicted water supply reduction in Africa by 2040.

....

....

....

[2]

b)   Using **Figure 5**, state how Malawi's crop yields are predicted to change by 2050. Suggest **one** possible cause of this change.

....

....

....

[2]

Decision-Making Exercise

c) Using **Figure 5** and your own knowledge, suggest how changing crop yields might affect food security in Africa by 2050.

....

....

....

....

[3]

d) Which of the countries in **Figure 6** is the least developed? Justify your answer using evidence from **Figure 6**.

Least developed country:...

....

....

....

[3]

e) To what extent do you agree that less developed countries will suffer the most from the effects of climate change? Use evidence from **Figures 3**, **4**, **5** and **6** and your own knowledge to justify your answer.

[12 + 3 SPaG]

[Total 25 marks]

3 Study **Figures 8**, **9**, **10** and **11** on pages 81-82, information about farming and changes in land use and photographs of life in Malawi.

a) **Figure 10** shows changes in areas of forest cover and agricultural land in Malawi between 1990 and 2013. By how many percentage points did forest cover decrease?

....

[1]

b) Use **Figures 8**, **9** and **11** to suggest reasons for the changing forest cover in Malawi.

....

....

....

....

....

....

....

[6]

[Total 7 marks]

Decision-Making Exercise

4   Study **Figures 1**, **6, 7**, and **9** on page 81, information about child nutrition and farming in Malawi.

a)   In 2010, there were 2.5 million children aged under 5 years old in Malawi, of whom 1.2 million suffered from chronic undernutrition. Calculate this as a percentage and plot it on **Figure 7**.

....

[2]

b)   Using evidence from **Figures 1**, **6** and **9**, suggest **two** reasons for the levels of undernutrition among children under 5 in Malawi shown in **Figure 7**.

....

....

....

....

....

[4]

[Total 6 marks]

5   Study **all** of the information on pages 80-82.

a)   "Increasing the area of land used for agriculture will increase food security in Malawi."
To what extent do you agree with this statement?
Give reasons for your answer using information from **Figures 1-12**.

....

....

....

....

....

....

....

....

....

[6]

b)   Using information from pages 80-82 and your own knowledge, write a report on food security in Malawi and decide on a strategy to increase food security there.
In your report you need to:
1.   Describe the current state of food security in Malawi including potential challenges for the country in the near future.
2.   Suggest and justify a sustainable strategy to increase food security in Malawi.

[12 + 3 SPaG]

[Total 21 marks]

Fieldwork

Fieldwork

1   Study **Figure 1**, a photograph of a housing estate in north east England, and **Figure 2**, a stream in the Lake District National Park.

Figure 1

Figure 2

a)   Suggest **one** question that could form the basis of a human geography enquiry in the area shown in **Figure 1**.

....

....
[1]

b)   Outline **one** primary data collection technique that could be used in the area shown in **Figure 1** to help answer this question.

....

....

....
[2]

c)   Outline **one** primary data collection technique that could be used in the area shown in **Figure 2** to investigate the relationship between river velocity and the formation of meanders.

....

....

....
[2]

d)   Suggest **one** possible risk of collecting data in the area shown in **Figure 2**.

....

....
[1]
[Total 6 marks]

Fieldwork

2   As part of a fieldwork enquiry, a student counted the number of walkers to pass a certain point on a footpath during a 10-minute period. She then measured the width of the footpath using a metre ruler. She repeated this at ten different points on the footpath. The results are shown in **Figure 3**.

a)   Complete the graph in **Figure 3** by adding the data for the final site, which was used by 16 walkers and measured 350 cm wide.
[1]

b)   Draw a line of best fit on the graph in **Figure 3**.
[1]

c)   Using **Figure 3**, predict the width of a stretch of footpath used by 26 walkers.

.... cm
[1]

Figure 3

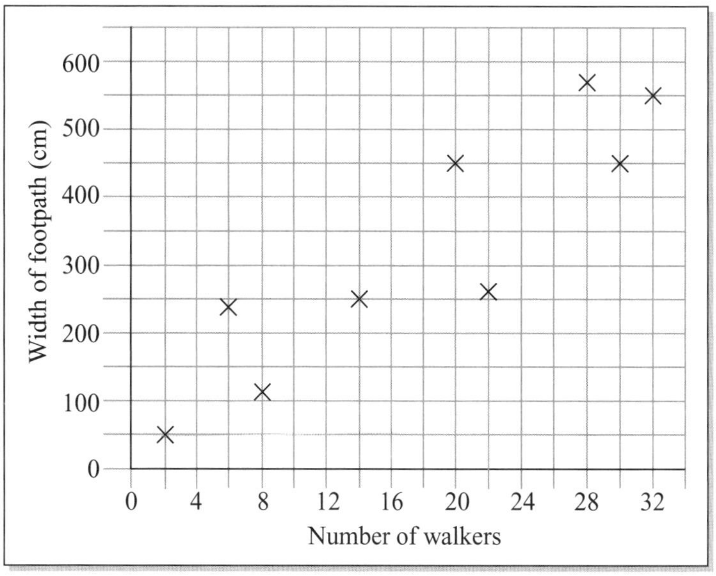

d)   Suggest **one** possible problem with the method used to measure the width of the footpath that might lead to inaccuracies in the data collected.

....

....

....
[2]

e)   Suggest **one** way in which the data collected on the number of walkers could be made more reliable.

....

....

....
[2]

f)   What conclusion might you draw about the impact of walkers on footpath erosion using the results shown in **Figure 3**?

....

....
[1]

g)   Give **one** source of secondary data that you could use to test this conclusion.

....

....
[1]

[Total 9 marks]

Fieldwork

3   A group of students sent a questionnaire to a random selection of residents in twenty districts in
Greaton. The results from one question for three of the districts are shown in **Figure 4**.
Figure 5 is a photo of a street in district Q and **Figure 6** is a map showing the percentage of
people in each district from ethnic minority groups.

Figure 4

Q1 *'To what extent has the city's
character been influenced by ethnic
diversity?' (1 = not very much,
4 = very strongly)*
Percentage of people giving each
score in districts A, E and Q:

		District		
		A	E	Q
Score	1	75	21	12
	2	10	7	2
	3	8	35	8
	4	7	37	78

Figure 5

Figure 6

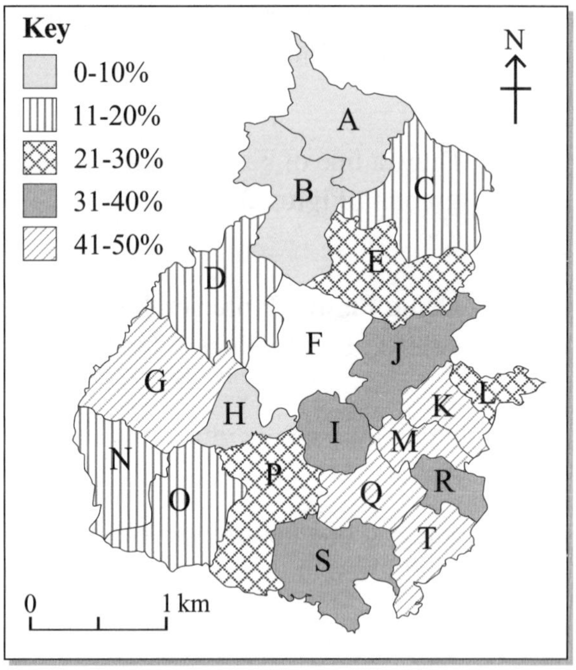

Key
☐ 0-10%
▥ 11-20%
▨ 21-30%
▦ 31-40%
▧ 41-50%

a)   What is the percentage range of people from
ethnic minority groups in district E?

    ....
                                                                  [1]

b)   Complete **Figure 6** to show that the proportion of ethnic minority groups in district F is 17%.
                                                                  [1]

c)   Describe the pattern of ethnic diversity in Greaton shown in **Figure 6**.

    ....

    ....

    ....

    ....

    ....
                                                                  [3]

d)   Suggest **one** other way in which the students could have presented the data shown in **Figure 6**.

    ....

    ....
                                                                  [1]

e)   The student's enquiry question was 'To what extent is ethnic diversity influencing the character of
Greaton?' Using evidence from **Figures 4**, **5** and **6**, write a conclusion to the investigation.
                                                                  [8 + 3 SPaG]

                                                                  [Total 17 marks]

Fieldwork

4   A student wanted to investigate how people's food shopping habits have changed over time. As part of his fieldwork enquiry, he collected data on the amount of organic food that people buy. The data was collected through a door-to-door survey in a village with an organic farm shop. The results are shown in **Figure 7**.

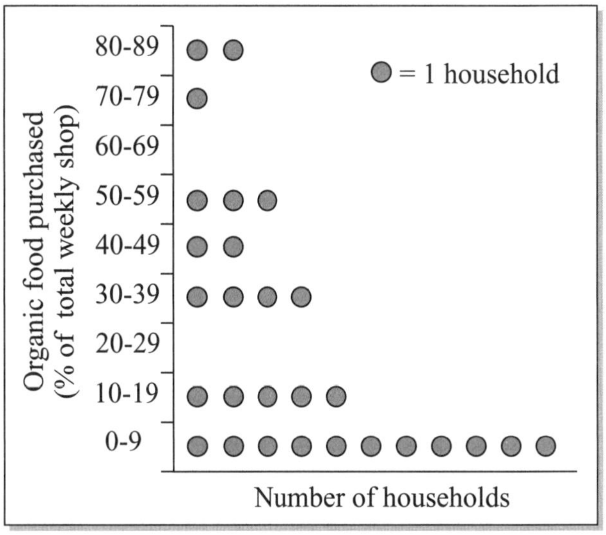

a)   Complete the graph to show that nine households in the survey buy 20-29% of their weekly shop from organic sources.

[1]

Figure 7

b)   What is the modal class of the data shown in **Figure 7**?

....

[1]

c)   Calculate the percentage of households whose weekly shop is 0-9% organic.

....

....

....

[2]

d)   Describe the results shown in **Figure 7**.

....

....

....

....

....

[3]

e)   Outline **one** limitation of the data collection technique used in this enquiry.

....

....

....

[2]

f)   Suggest **one** other source of primary data that may be useful in this enquiry.

....

....

....

[2]

[Total 11 marks]

Fieldwork

5   A student wanted to investigate how wave characteristics affect the cross-profile of a beach.
    Figure 8 shows the method she used to find the cross-profile of the beach. She measured
    the profile at three points along the beach. The results are shown in **Figure 9**.

Figure 8

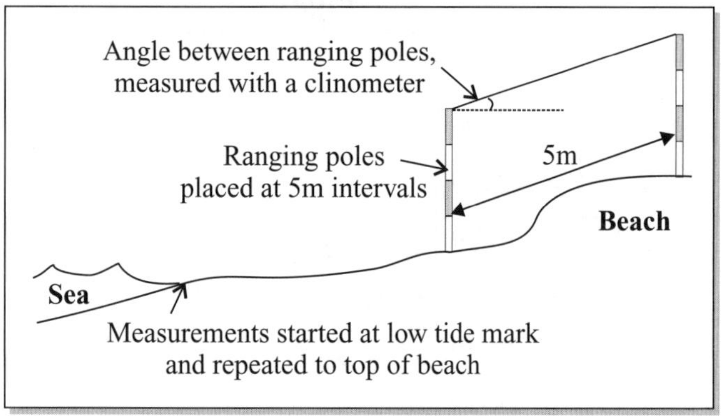

Figure 9

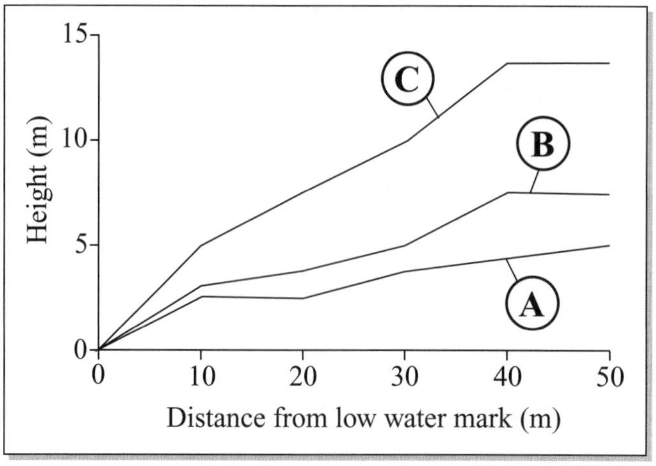

a)   Describe **two** possible sources of
     inaccuracy in the method used.

     Source 1: ....

     ....

     Source 2: ....

     ....

     [2]

b)   Suggest **one** way in which the reliability of the data could be improved.

     ....

     ....

     ....

     [2]

c)   Suggest **one** way in which the student could add to **Figure 9** so that the data is presented
     more effectively.

     ....

     ....

     ....

     [2]

d)   Suggest **one** other source of primary data that the student could collect to help her answer the
     research question.

     ....

     ....

     [1]

     [Total 7 marks]

Fieldwork

6 As part of a fieldwork enquiry, a student collected data on river velocity.
He placed a float in the river and recorded the time taken for the float to
travel 10 metres downstream. The results are shown in **Figure 10**.

Figure 10

Sample	Time (s)
1	315
2	255
3	278
4	310
5	947
6	302
7	279
8	297

a) Suggest **one** appropriate item that could be used as the float.
Give **one** reason for your answer.

Item:..
[1]

Reason: ....

....

....
[1]

b) Which sample in the data is an anomaly?

....

[1]

c) Suggest **one** possible reason for the anomaly.

....

....

....

[2]

d) Excluding the anomaly, calculate the **median** time taken for the float to travel 10 m.

....

....

Median = ... s
[2]

e) Excluding the anomaly, calculate the **mean** time taken for the float to travel 10 m.

....

....

Mean = ... s
[2]

f) Excluding the anomaly, calculate the interquartile range of the data shown in **Figure 10**.

....

....

Interquartile range = ...
[2]

[Total 11 marks]

Fieldwork

Fieldwork Enquiry

1   This question is about your fieldwork enquiry that involved the collection of **physical geography** data.

You might not have completed your fieldwork yet — don't start this section until your enquiry is finished.

a)   Justify **one** of the primary data collection techniques that you used.

Primary data collection technique:...

Justification: ....

....

....

....

[3]

b)   Outline **two** strengths of **one** of the data presentation techniques that you used.

Data presentation technique:...

Strength 1:...

....

....

Strength 2:...

....

....

[4]

c)   Describe the patterns shown in **one** of your sets of data.

Data set:..

Patterns:..

....

....

....

[3]

d)   Outline **one** limitation of the primary data you collected.

....

....

[1]

e)   To what extent did your results allow you to reach a valid conclusion to your original question?

[8 + 3 SPaG]

[Total 22 marks]

Fieldwork Enquiry

2   This question is about your fieldwork enquiry that involved the collection of **human geography** data.

a)   Describe **one** primary data collection technique you used and explain why you used it.

Primary data collection technique:..

Description and explanation:..

....

....

....

[3]

b)   Justify the data presentation technique(s) you used.

....

....

....

....

....

....

[4]

c)   Outline **one** way in which your data collection methods could have been improved.

....

....

....

[2]

d)   Outline how your fieldwork enquiry improved your understanding of an area of geography.

....

....

....

....

[3]

e)   Assess the effectiveness of your data collection methods in helping you to answer your original question.

[8 + 3 SPaG]

[Total 23 marks]

Fieldwork

Acknowledgements

Map of drought risk on p.10 © 'UCL Global Drought Monitor'.

Graph of tiltmeter readings Mount St Helens on p.16 © Earth Science Australia 1995-2009. www.earthsci.org

Data used to construct the graph of sulfur dioxide emissions at Mt St Helens on p.16 © U.S. Geological Survey, www.usgs.gov

Graph on p.19: global annual average near-surface temperature anomalies (difference from 1961-1990 average). Data from HadCRUT.4.4.0.0 which is produced by the Met Office Hadley Centre in collaboration with the University of East Anglia Climatic Research Unit.

Graph of sea level rise on p.20 adapted from Climate Change 2001: The Scientific Basis. Contribution of Working Group I to the Third Assessment Report of the Intergovernmental Panel on Climate Change. Figure 5. Cambridge University Press.

With thanks to © iStock.com for images on pages 25, 30, 32, 39, 41, 53 and 82.

Map extracts on pages 26 and 29 reproduced with permission by Ordnance Survey® © Crown copyright 2016 OS 100034841

Photograph on p.2 and p.31 (V-shaped valley) © Anne Burgess / p.2 and p.31 (River Lune) © Michael Fox / p.27 (coastal erosion) © Stephen McKay / p.27 (South West Coast Path) © David Smith / p.56 (damaged building in Libya) © Al Jazeera English / p.67 (central London) © Colin Smith / p.69 (film set) © Jake Watson / p.70 (road in Harrow) © David Hawgood / p.70 (parade in Omagh) © Kenneth Allen / p.70 (shops in Coventry) © Jaggery / p.72 (tractor spraying chemicals) © Hugh Venables / p.78 (shops in Todmorden) © Richard Dorrell / p.86 (housing estate) © Trevor Littlewood / p.88 (street) © Stephen McKay. Licensed for re-use under the Creative Commons Attribution-Share Alike 2.0 Generic Licence. https://creativecommons.org/licenses/by-sa/2.0/

Data used to construct urban population graph on p.45 from World Bank Staff estimates based on United Nations, World Urbanization Prospects.

Population table on p.47 adapted from United Nations, Department of Economic and Social Affairs, Population Division (2014). World Urbanization Prospects: The 2014 Revision, Highlights (ST/ESA/SER.A/352).

Population data in table on p.50 source: NOMIS, population estimates.

Business start up data in table on p.50 source: ONS, Business Demography, NOMIS, Mid-year population estimates.

Migration graph on p.51; population graph on p.52; house prices line in housing graph on p.52; population density of the UK map on p.62; 2001 population graph on p.63; map on p.65 all adapted from data from the Office for National Statistics. Graph of housing completions on p.52 based on DCLG live table on house building 253. Information used in article on p.61 provided by Department for International Development. Table on p.64 adapted from data from the Office for National Statistics, National Records of Scotland, Northern Ireland Statistics and Research Agency. All contain public sector information licensed under the Open Government Licence v3.0. http://www.nationalarchives.gov.uk/doc/open-government-licence/version/3/

Statistics on p.54 (except GNI and HDI); data used to calculate GDP change on p.56; UK birth and death rates on p.63; population, employment and GDP data in Figure 8 on p.81 from The World Factbook. Washington, DC: Central Intelligence Agency, 2016

GNI per capita values on p.54 and data in table on p.81 (except HDI and World Hunger Index) from The World Bank: Indicators

HDI values on p.54 and p.81 from 2015 Human Development Report, United Nations Development Programme from hdr.undp.org. Licensed under the Creative Commons Attribution 3.0 IGO license. http://creativecommons.org/licenses/by/3.0/igo/

Data used to construct map of ACs, LIDCs and EDCs on p.55 from The World Bank: Country and Lending Groups.

Data used to compile the graphs on p.57 © World Trade Organization 2016. http://stat.wto.org/CountryProfile/WSDBCountryPFReporter.aspx?Language=E

Land use map on p.62 based on: Cole, B.; King, S.; Ogutu, B.; Palmer, D.; Smith, G.; Balzter, H. (2015). Corine land cover 2012 for the UK, Jersey and Guernsey. NERC Environmental Information Data Centre. (http://doi.org/10.5285/32533dd6-7c1b-43e1-b892-e80d61a5ea1d.) This resource is made available under the terms of the Open Government Licence.

2015 population pyramid on p.63 constructed using data from Population Division, World Population Prospects, the 2015 revision, by Department of Economic and Social Affairs. © United Nations 2016. Accessed 23.06.2016. Reprinted with the permission of the United Nations.

Graph on p.66 adapted from Welsh Government - Statistics © Crown Copyright 2015

Table on p.69 source: The Numbers, http://www.the-numbers.com/movie/Skyfall#tab=international

Cereal production map on p.74 © FAO 2016 Cereal production quantities by country 2012 -2014 http://faostat3.fao.org/browse/Q/QC/E 11.03.2016 This is an adaptation of an original work by FAO.

Calorie intake map on p.75 and data used to construct UK calorie intake graph on p.79 © FAO 2016 World food supply 2011-2013 http://faostat3.fao.org/browse/FB/FBS/E 09.09.2016

Data used to construct graph on p.76 from Eurostat © European Union, 1995-2016.

Water supply map on p.80: Luck, M., M. Landis, F. Gassert. 2015. "Aqueduct Water Stress Projections: Decadal projections of water supply and demand using CMIP5 GCMs." Washington, DC: World Resources Institute. Licensed under a Creative Commons Attribution International 4.0 License.

Change in crop yields map on p.80: The World Bank: Change in Agriculture Yields: Climate Change Knowledge Portal

Global Hunger Index values and undernutrition graph on page 81: von Grebmer, K., J. Bernstein, A. de Waal, N. Prasai, S. Yin, and Y. Yohannes. 2015. 2015 Global Hunger Index: Armed Conflict and the Challenge of Hunger. "Bangladesh, Malawi, and Prevalence of Stunting in Children Under Five Years (%)." Bonn: Welthungerhilfe; Washington, DC: International Food Policy Research Institute; Concern Worldwide: Dublin. http://ghi.ifpri.org/.

Figure 10 on p.82: Food and Agriculture Organization, electronic files and web site.

Every effort has been made to locate copyright holders and obtain permission to reproduce sources. For those sources where it has been difficult to trace the copyright holder of the work, we would be grateful for information. If any copyright holder would like us to make an amendment to the acknowledgements, please notify us and we will gladly update the book at the next reprint. Thank you.